42:

DISCOVERING FAITH THROUGH FANDOM

ERIC ANDERSON

NATHAN MARCHAND

Interior Design by Nathan Marchand
Cover and Artwork by Ruth Pike

First Printing

Eric:
To Dr. Doug Barcalow, for giving me good
foundations on spiritual formations and curriculum
development. This book wouldn't be possible
without your classes!

Nathan:
To Dr. Dennis E. "Doc" Hensley, who taught me
how to write many things, including devotions. This
book wouldn't exist without your tutelage. And to
his wife, Rose Hensley, whose hospitality and
amazing cooking gave Doc's students much-needed
respites and reminded them how much they were
loved.

Day 1: The Ultimate Question of Life, the Universe, and Everything
By Nathan Marchand

Now all has been heard;
here is the conclusion of the matter:
Fear God and keep his commandments,
for this is the duty of all mankind.
For God will bring every deed into judgment,
including every hidden thing,
whether it is good or evil.
Ecclesiastes 12:13-14

In one chapter of the classic book *The Hitchhiker's Guide to the Galaxy,* Douglas Adams satirizes the search for the meaning of life. An ancient race constructs a massive super-computer (the second best in the universe), named Deep Thought, to tell them what it is. Unfortunately, Deep Thought has to think about it. How long? Seven-and-a-half million years. (And you thought Windows ME was slow.) So, after that race waits in eager anticipation...

"All right," said Deep Thought. "The Answer to the Great Question..."

"Yes...!"

"Of Life, the Universe, and Everything..." said Deep Thought.

"Yes...!"

"Is..." said Deep Thought, and paused.

"Yes...!!!..?"

"Forty-two."

A few minutes later, after some angry questioning, Deep Thought added, "Once you know what the question actually is, you'll know what the answer means."

Many of you reading this book already know the question and have been waiting for what seems like 7.5 million years searching for your own "Answer." Or you may have even believed you've found it. Perhaps you've read much on religion and philosophy (we nerds love to read). Perhaps you've lost yourself in your hobbies—cosplay, LARP-ing, comics, etc.—hoping they would bring you fulfillment. But you still feel empty.

I'm here to tell you there *is* an Answer. And you don't need to build the second-greatest supercomputer in the universe to find it.

Strangely enough, even Douglas Adams—a "devout" atheist—hinted at the Answer in the prologue of the same book:

> *And then, one Thursday, nearly two thousand years after one man had been nailed to a tree for saying how great it would be to be nice to people for a change...*

Yes, True Believers (as Stan Lee would say), the Answer is Jesus Christ.

But Deep Thought's answer of "42" won't be ignored. Later in that book, some characters theorized what the Question might be, with suggestions like, "How many paths must a young man walk?" In your case, perhaps it could be, "How many days will it take me to learn the Truth?" That's why this devotional is 42 days long.

Like the famous Guide, we're here to tell you, *Don't Panic*. Think of that as the nerd equivalent of the Bible's oft-quoted phrase, "Fear not." Eric and I are lifelong nerds, and we believe that Truth with a capital T can be found in all nerds'/geeks' favorite hobbies and stories. You just have to look hard enough. Perhaps that's why many of us bury ourselves in them: we're trying to find that elusive Truth.

The 42-day journey you are about to undertake will be a harrowing-but-exciting one; one that will change you forever, whether you're seeking Truth or want to deepen your faith.

Don't forget your towel!

Quest of the Day

1. Read Ecclesiastes 12.
2. In what ways have you tried to answer "the question" in your own life? List them. How did they not satisfy?

Day 2: Ordinary but Extraordinary
By Eric Anderson

My ears had heard of you but now my eyes have seen you.
Job 42:5a

It was a normal day. Moses was taking care of his sheep and looking for a lost one…when he came across a bush. It was on fire, but not burning. Paul was traveling from Jerusalem up to Damascus when he experienced the unthinkable…a bright flash of light that blinded him, and a loud voice that only he could understand. For Job, it happened in the middle of hopelessness. His children and servants were dead, and his crops and livestock were stolen and destroyed. He was significantly ill. What do they have in common? They all had conversations with the Most High God.

Even in our modern, fictional narratives we realize that most days are normal, but some days are strange. An experience. Luke Skywalker meets Obi-Wan Kenobi after searching for a lost droid and holds this weird thing called a lightsaber. Lucy walks into a wardrobe during a game of hide and seek, only to find a whole new world inside. Amelia Pond wakes up in the middle of the night to find a madman with a blue box in her garden. Arthur's house and planet are demolished, but he wakes up in a spaceship.

4

We want this. We want interesting, new experiences. We need the normal, too, but we crave those ordinary days when something extraordinary happens.

Over the next forty days, I hope you have experiences; not void of learning, but transcending it. I don't want you to only learn more about God or the Bible. I want you to experience the Risen Christ.

Who is this Risen Christ, you ask?

"He is the image of the invisible God, the firstborn over all creation. For by him all things were created: things in heaven and on earth, visible and invisible, whether thrones or powers or rulers or authorities; all things were created by him and for him. He is before all things, and in him all things hold together" (Colossians 1:15-17).

Yes, it is a little scary. Maybe you feel a little nervous. Could that be a good thing? Nervousness that comes from stepping out of a comfort zone to find something deep, true, and new is not a bad thing. Sometimes those nerve-wracking experiences are what we need.

There will be days when you have more reading. Other days you'll be asked to simply pray and wait in silence for a few minutes. God listens when we pray...but He also speaks through His Word, the Holy Spirit, and other experiences. You will have "quests" to complete to help you seek out the larger journey of experiencing and serving the Messiah Himself.

If you've already grabbed your towel, then get a lightsaber, a Bible, and some Elven bread, because this is going to be an adventure!

Quest of the Day

1. Ask Jesus to reveal Himself to you. Spend a few minutes in silence.
2. Read Luke 6. Then write down two questions and a few thoughts (related or unrelated to the questions).

DAY 3: THE PRESSURE OF PROPHECY
BY ERIC ANDERSON

Father, if you are willing, take this cup from me; yet not my
will, but yours be done.
Luke 22:42

Some think that it was only his love for Padme that
made Anakin turn to the dark side of the Force. You could
also argue that it was power alone, with that attachment as a
chance to use power. I wonder if there was another aspect,
though. At one point in *Revenge of the Sith*, Obi-Wan tells
Anakin, "You were supposed to destroy the Sith, not join
them!" He was referring to a prophecy that someone would
bring balance to the Force. Anakin had been trained with
knowledge of this prophecy, perhaps once in a while being
told he was supposed to fulfill it and save everything. Could
you handle that pressure? Would you crack under it and seek
the power of the Dark Side, especially if you thought your
wife was going to die?

Jesus had a lot of pressure on Him. His name means
"God saves," and He knew what He was supposed to do.
Why else would He be in such pain in Gethsemane as He
prayed before being arrested? His goal was to take all the sin
of the universe, throughout all time and space, on His
shoulders; to take all that punishment. He had been offered a

way out about three years earlier. "Serve me," said Lucifer, after Jesus had been fasting for 40 days, when his body was weak. He offered to give the whole world to Jesus. But Jesus knew there was a different plan in the works; a way to save the world, not just control it. Several times He tried to tell His disciples about this plan.

"We are going up to Jerusalem, and everything that is written by the prophets about the Son of Man will be fulfilled. He will be handed over to the Gentiles. They will mock him, insult him, spit on him, flog him, and kill him" (Luke 18:31, 32).

This doesn't sound like a fun plan, does it? What had the prophets said? Jesus was going to fulfill the role of the Suffering Servant.

"He grew up before him like a tender shoot, and like a root out of dry ground. He had no beauty or majesty to attract us to him, nothing in his appearance that we should desire him. He was despised and rejected by men, a man of sorrows, and familiar with suffering. Like one from whom men hide their faces he was despised, and we esteemed him not. Surely he took up our infirmities and carried our sorrows, yet we considered him stricken by God, smitten by him, and afflicted. But he was pierced for our transgressions, he was crushed for our iniquities, the punishment that brought us peace was upon him, and by his wounds we are healed" (Isaiah 53:2-5).

The good news, the Gospel, the exciting thing is...*Jesus did not crack!* All that pressure. All that suffering. The crucifixion was such a painful form of death. So painful they created a new word to describe the pain (the basis for our word "excruciating"). Jesus endured it.

"Let us fix our eyes on Jesus, the author and perfecter of our faith, who for the joy set before him endured the cross, scorning its shame, and sat down at the right had of the throne of God. Consider him who endured such opposition from sinful men, so that you will not grow weary and lose heart" (Hebrews 12:2, 3).

"Consider" Him. Think about Him. Remember Jesus as you go through each day; each painful, difficult, dreary day. Are you willing to trust someone who endured painful torture for you?

Quest of the Day

1. Think about the pressures you face each day. The big ones, the little ones. Pray and ask Jesus for help. Ask Him for wisdom, strength, and mercy. Mention each issue and ask for specific help with it.

2. Think about someone who is under a lot of pressure. Send him a note of encouragement. Pray for him.

DAY 4: LEARNING TO BE HUMAN
BY NATHAN MARCHAND

"You will be with child and give birth to a son, and you are to give him the name Jesus"…
"How will this be," Mary asked the angel, "since I am a virgin?"
The angel answered, "The Holy Spirit will come upon you, and the power of the Most High will overshadow you. So the holy one to be born will be called the Son of God."
Luke 1:31, 34-35

Star Trek is overly-fond of disembodied aliens. No doubt it was originally to save on special effects costs, but it eventually became a staple.

When *Star Trek: The Next Generation* started, this tradition continued. The first episode of its second season, "The Child," while considered by many to be a bad episode (and understandably so), takes this concept in an interesting direction. An alien being made of energy enters the body of Deanna Troi—the Enterprise-D's half-human/half-Betazoid counselor—and she becomes pregnant. The baby grows quickly, and she gives birth within a few days. The child is a human/Betazoid hybrid like his "mother," and Troi names him Ian.

But Ian grows just as fast outside the womb, becoming a boy of age seven or eight within a few days. He does things like intentionally burning his hand on a pan. Troi talks with him and learns that he did what he did to experience what it was like to be human, which included negative experiences like pain.

The Enterprise is transporting samples of a plague to a medical station, and it's learned that a strange radiation is causing the virus to expand and grow, which will eventually rupture the containment unit, threatening the entire ship. The radiation is traced back to Ian, so he lets himself "die" or rather, revert to his true form, and leaves the ship to save everyone; but not before thanking Troi for a wonderful experience.

Despite the story's potentially controversial elements (was Troi "raped"?), rarely in fiction has there been a story with such striking parallels to the birth of Jesus Christ. Like Ian, Jesus was born through what theologians call "immaculate conception." In other words, while He was born through a human mother, He had no human father. He was conceived by the Holy Spirit. This was done so that He would be free of the sinful nature that has plagued mankind since Adam and Eve disobeyed God. It made Him unique. It showed He truly was the Messiah. He had the credentials.

Also, believe it or not, Jesus did want to experience what it was like to be human, just like Ian. "For we do not have a high priest who is unable to sympathize with our weaknesses, but we have one who has been tempted in every way, just as we are—yet was without sin" (Hebrews 4:15). The God of the universe, Who Himself was spirit, became flesh. He experienced firsthand our temptations and struggles. More than ever, He understood what it was like to be human. Can you imagine the boy Jesus bruising His knee while playing? Finally, like Ian, Jesus died to save others.

Strange how even a less-than-great episode of *TNG* holds great truth within it.

Jesus is not a distant God. He understands what it is like to be human, because He became human! He knows our triumphs and tragedies, our joys and sorrows. He did it all without sinning, yet it wasn't always easy. Read about His temptation in the wilderness or His anguish in Gethsemane, and you'll see how hard it was for Him. But He did it all because He loves us.

That puts every episode of *Star Trek* to shame.

Quest of the Day

1. Read Matthew 1:18-25 and Luke 1:38, 2:1-20.
2. If you were Joseph or Mary, how would you react to being the parents of the Son of God? Ponder this and then journal about it.

DAY 5: HEALING POWER OF CHRIST
BY ERIC ANDERSON

Jesus went throughout Galilee, teaching in their synagogues,
proclaiming the good news of the kingdom, and healing every
disease and sickness among the people.
Mathew 4:23

In the movie version of *The Lion, the Witch, and the
Wardrobe*, Lucy Pevensie was given a vial by Father Christmas.
This vial was said to be made of diamond and contained a
juice from a flower said to be found on the Sun. It was a
healing juice. She later used it after the battle with the White
Witch to heal not only her brother Edmund from a nearly-
deadly wound, but many others wounded in that battle. I'm
sure that was a long day.

Jesus had many long days. Often, He would go to
towns to preach and heal, and people would keep crowding
around Him again and again. One of those days was at his
disciple Peter's house. Peter's mother-in-law was sick in bed
with a fever. He held her hand, rebuked the fever, and she
immediately was healed and got up to start waiting on Jesus
and his friends. That evening, people started coming from
around the town. In fact, the whole town gathered at the
door. Many were brought to Jesus who were sick or demon-
possessed.

Another day is recorded where Jesus decided to sail across the lake. First, they experienced a sudden storm and Jesus rebuked it. Next, they met a demoniac. Jesus sent the demons into pigs, which then committed mass suicide in the lake. Jesus then returned back to the first side of the lake and did more healing. A man named Jairus came and asked Jesus to heal his daughter. On the way to Jairus' house, a woman grabbed at Jesus' garment. She was immediately healed! As Jesus was talking with her, servants came to say that the daughter had died, but Jesus went on to the house anyway and raised her from the dead.

There was one key thing that Jesus often said: "Your faith has healed you." When I was in a discipleship training school with YWAM (Youth with a Mission), I had to come to terms with my own fear of miracles. I was actually more afraid of them than I thought. Not that I didn't believe in them; more like I was really nervous about the issue. Later, I experienced a personal healing from Christ. I was in Jordan teaching English for eight weeks. In the last week, I was going down to give the exams, but I had a headache. I prayed and asked God for healing. In the middle of the first exam, my headache went away. That night I gave two exams, and graded all the exams from the first class.

How do *you* need healing? Are you emotionally scarred? Physically hurt? Start praying. God does not always choose miraculous routes to heal, but He often does; more often than we scientifically-minded Americans like to think. Imagine if Lucy had refused to believe that the potion would work and ignored it.

Quest of the Day

1. Do your own research by looking through the Gospels and read up on Jesus' healing miracles.
2. Pray for yourself or someone else who needs healing.

DAY 6: THE MAN OF STEEL
BY NATHAN MARCHAND

For in Christ all the fullness of the Deity lives in bodily form.
Colossians 2:9

"Faster than a speeding bullet. More powerful than a locomotive. Able to leap tall buildings in a single bound. This amazing stranger from the planet Krypton. The man of steel—Superman!"

This was part of the theme song to all the Superman cartoons produced by Fleischer Studios in the 1940s. It has since become not only an integral part of Supes' mythos, but a part of Americana. What kid didn't grow up hearing those words? Many of the boys who did grabbed the nearest bath towel, tied it around their necks, and jumped from the kitchen counter in an attempt to fly. (I know I did.)

Superman is a character capable of incredible feats no mortal can do. Indeed, he almost seems capable of inventing whatever superpowers he needs at that moment to save the day (like the ability to fire rainbows from his fingers…I'll leave it at that). His trademark powers include flight, super-strength, x-ray vision, super-speed, heat vision, and super-breath. He's been known to move entire planets (see the finale of *Smallville*) or spin the world backward (see *Superman:*

The Movie). Many people in the DC Comics universe have come to describe him as a god.

Superman: The Movie goes a step further. Just before launching Kal-El (Superman) in a spaceship to avoid the destruction of Krypton, his father, Jor-El, says this to him: "They could be a great people, Kal-El. They wish to be. They lack only the light to show the way. For this reason above all, their capacity for good, I am sending them you, my only son." Superman was sent to Earth to use his powers to save mankind.

Doesn't that sound like Jesus Christ?

Many people nowadays think of Jesus as just another teacher and philosopher. He was good and wise, but still a mere mortal. They're either ignorant of some of Jesus' teachings or they disregard them.

"'I tell you the truth,' Jesus answered, 'before Abraham was, I AM!" (John 8:58). ("I AM" was the name God, in the form of the burning bush, told Moses to tell the Israelites when they asked which god had sent him).

"I and the Father are one" (John 10:30).

"Anyone who has seen me has seen the Father" (John 14:9).

These are just a few verses where Jesus claims to be divine.

But it doesn't stop there. As we discussed yesterday, Jesus performed miracles unlike anything people had seen. He healed the sick (Matthew 8:16-17); He made the blind see (Matthew 9:27-31); He exorcised demons (Mark 1:21-27); He raised the dead (John 11:1-45). In fact, in one story, a woman was healed by simply touching the edge of Jesus' clothes (Luke 8:26-39). However, His greatest miracle was rising from the grave on the first Easter morning (Matthew 28:1-10).

He has every right to call Himself God.

C.S. Lewis wrote in *Mere Christianity* that, in light of all this, only three conclusions can be drawn: Jesus was either a liar, a lunatic, or the Lord.

Which do you think He is?

Quest of the Day

1. Ponder Lewis' proposition: Do you think Jesus is a lair, a lunatic, or the Lord? Journal about it. Could He be anything else?

2. What is so difficult in your life right now you need a *God* to save you from it or to help you with it? Write it down and spend time in prayer about it.

DAY 7: THE MILD-MANNERED REPORTER
BY NATHAN MARCHAND

And Jesus grew in wisdom and stature, and in favor with God
and men.
Luke 2:52

"Superman fights a never-ending battle for truth and
justice disguised as a mild-mannered newspaper reporter,
Clark Kent," says the announcer at the end of the theme for
Fleischer Studios' Superman cartoons.

Yet nobody ever suspects Clark is Superman (it's
amazing what a simple pair of eyeglasses can hide for over 75
years). No surprise. They're nothing alike. Superman is a tall,
strong, confident superhero. Clark Kent isn't "super" at all.
He's just a Kansas farm boy who moved to the big city and
became a reporter. Some stories even present Clark as a
bumbling buffoon (à la Christopher Reeve).

But in most versions of the Superman story,
Superman is just the public persona. Clark Kent is who he
really is. In many retellings, Clark never puts the costume on
until he was close to 30 years old! He was Clark Kent growing
up, not Superman.

People in the DC universe admire him, perhaps even
idolize him, but it's doubtful they relate to him. All those

19

powers, all those adventures. He is so far above them he may as well be a god.

But *everyone* can identify with Clark Kent. He works a nine-to-five job. He has to deal with an annoying boss. He's in love with a woman he can't summon the courage to talk to. Who hasn't dealt with stuff like that?

I would argue that, without Clark Kent, Superman wouldn't be super. The Man of Steel is who he is because of his upbringing. If he hadn't been raised by the down-to-earth and moralistic Jonathan and Martha Kent, he may have grown up into the world's greatest enemy and not its hero (play the video game *Injustice: Gods Among Us* to see what I mean). In fact, it isn't the powers that make Superman a hero. In an issue of the comic series *52*, Clark Kent, who had recently lost his powers, jumps out a window to attract the attention of a new superhero so he can score an interview. That takes heroic courage!

While many in the secular world deny Jesus' divinity, many Christians are guilty of the opposite: they emphasize Jesus' divinity to the point of dehumanizing Him. They fail to see that by doing so, they have an incomplete picture of who He is.

Jesus became human so that we could be reconciled to God. Before Christ came, God had a personal, yet intangible, relationship with His people. He was a voice from the heavens, a pillar of fire, a burning bush. Moses asked to see God once, but he was shown only the Lord's back. Then Jesus came. People walked with Him, talked with Him, ate with Him. The God of the universe became one of us! He experienced the same struggles we face daily, as Hebrews 4:15 says: "For we do not have a high priest who is unable to sympathize with our weaknesses, but we have one that has been tempted in every way, just as we are—yet was without sin."

Clark Kent and Superman are integral parts of the same character. Jesus Christ is fully divine *and* fully human. If He wasn't, He would cease to be mankind's Savior.

Quest of the Day

1. What struggles are you having that you fear no one will understand? Write them down. Then spend time in prayer about them.

2. Do you feel like no one gets you because you're "weird" or "odd"? Read Matthew 9:16-19 and Luke 7:31-35. Jesus was a "weirdo," too. Spend a little time in prayer talking to Him about your weirdness.

DAY 8: DO YOU *KNOW OF* OR *KNOW* THE DOCTOR?
BY NATHAN MARCHAND

They worship me in vain; their teachings are but rules taught
by men.
Matthew 15:9

Rose Tyler was having a weird day. Mannequins came to life and tried to kill her at work, but she was saved by a fast-talking man with a northern accent (because lots of planets have a north) who called himself "the Doctor." Then the shop exploded. She did what most Millennials do: sought answers on the Internet. Finding a website dedicated to the enigmatic Doctor, she arranged to meet the site's proprietor, Clive.

Clive took Rose to his basement (or, as some of us might call it, his "nerd cave") where he keeps everything he has on the Doctor: newspaper clippings, antique artwork, etc. The Doctor was present at President Kennedy's assassination and hung out with 19th century British aristocrats—yet he hadn't aged a day!

"The Doctor is a legend woven throughout history," Clive says. "When disaster comes, he's there. He brings a storm in his wake, and he only has one constant companion."

"What's that?" asks Rose.

"Death."

Clive goes on to tell her, "If he's singled you out, if the Doctor's making house calls…then God help you."

Later, she meets the Doctor again, and he saves her from a living plastic duplicate of her boyfriend. He then takes her on a trip in his ship, the TARDIS, which looks like a police call box and is bigger on the inside than it is on the outside. They embark on a harrowing adventure, where they save the world from the Autons—aliens made of living plastic. Throughout it all, she learns Clive's paranoid ideas were only partially true. The Doctor isn't a crazed killer. A lunatic for sure (he is, as he says a few seasons later, a madman with a blue box), but no killer.

Afterward, the Doctor asks Rose to go traveling with him. You can probably guess she said, "Yes."

In the New Testament, you can read how Jesus was frequently opposed by the Pharisees, a faction within the Jewish religion. They were sticklers for the ancient laws given to Moses by God. The problem was that they lost sight of God. They'd reduced faith to following rules. Not only that, but they supplemented the laws with traditions that overburdened people.

The Pharisees said they were true believers. Indeed, they knew much about God. They'd probably memorized most of the Hebrew Scriptures since they were children. But they didn't *know* God.

Jesus, on the other hand, wanted to bring people closer to God. He wanted them to know God as Father, like He did. He wanted them to have a relationship with God. "I came that they may have life, and have it to the full," he said (John 10:10b). He even went so far as to say, "Anyone who has seen me has seen the Father" (John 14:9b). Through Jesus, and only Jesus, we can go to the Father (John 14:6).

Clive *knew about* the Doctor. Rose *knew* the Doctor. Clive's knowledge led him to believe the Doctor was a harbinger of death. Rose learned from the Doctor himself that he wanted to save the Earth.

The same could be said of the Pharisees' perception of God and Jesus' relationship with God. Pharisees memorized laws. Jesus spent time alone with the Lawgiver.

And just like the Doctor did with Rose, Jesus is offering everyone the trip of a lifetime.

Quest of the Day

1. Read Matthew 23 and John 14.
2. Reflect on whether you know of God or know Him. Spend some time alone with Him. Journal about it.

DAY 9: OUR HAVEN
BY ERIC ANDERSON

This man was handed over to you by God's deliberate plan
and foreknowledge; and you, with the help of wicked men,
put him to death by nailing him to a cross.
Acts 2:23

It had been a long night and it was early in the
morning. He had been questioned, beaten, spat on, and
falsely accused. He had been on trial before the Sanhedrin
(the ruling council of the Jews) and before a governor and a
king. Now he was carrying a cross. His cross. He was being
treated like a thief or a murderer. In fact, two thieves were
walking the same path with him. Eventually, he fell to the
ground, weary from the torture. The soldiers had a man from
Cyrene carry Jesus' cross the rest of the way, but he still had
to walk.

Golgatha. The place of the Skull. A hill outside the
gates of the city. This was His morbid destination. He had
known this was coming, and Jesus, King of the Jews, as the
sign above His head would read, was ready for this. He had
prayed late into the night, filled with pain at what needed to
happen. After He had been hanging on the cross for a long
time, He felt a disturbance in His spirit. Surely more powerful
than the disturbance Yoda felt when many Jedi were killed at

Order 66. He cried out *"Eloi, eloi, lama sabachthani?"*, which means, "My God, My God, why have you forsaken me?"

In that moment, Jesus experienced a greater separation from God than you and I can ever know. In that moment, Jesus took on all sin from all of time and space. This death was painful. Nails in his hands and feet. Torture beforehand. A crown of thorns pressed onto his head. The rejection that came just hours before, when the people chose a criminal instead of Him for release from the shame of the cross.

Yet there was purpose in it.

He was redeeming the world. Substitutionary atonement. He was dying for us.

"You see, at just the right time, when we were still powerless, Christ died for the ungodly." (Romans 5:6)

"He is the atoning sacrifice for our sins, and not only for ours, but also for the whole world." (1 John 2:2)

Jesus died for others. Not for Himself. He could have walked away, as He had done before when His own hometown had tried to stone him. But He had a plan; a plan to save the world.

All the sacrifices Israel had done for thousands of years had led to this. They had pointed to this day. On the Day of Atonement, the high priest would sprinkle blood from sacrifices on the atonement cover on the Ark of the

Covenant. This happened every year. But Jesus was sinless. He could be the sacrifice Himself, but one that would last into eternity. In order for this to pan out, God chose to forsake Him on the cross. Jesus, 100% God and 100% man, accepted death to make atonement for us permanent.

In the show *Haven*, many of the townspeople have troubles that come upon them. These are often powers that affect those around them, such as the girl who changes weather with her emotions. Or something that inhibits the people, such as the families where the men have to move underwater because they go from breathing air to needing to be in water. Audrey Parker is immune to the effects. Every time the troubles come, she can choose to go into a barn. That "barn" amplifies her love, thereby holding the troubles at bay. But after time, she needs to recharge her love, so she comes out of the barn and the troubles come back. There is only one way she could stop this continuous, endless cycle of the barn: someone she loves must die. So appalled at the thought of this, she always chooses to go back into the barn. She chooses to leave her loved ones, instead of saving thousands forever by the death of one of them.

God made a different choice. He chose to end the continuous cycle of sin and animal sacrifice, to provide power for us to change our ways and grow in Him, by the death of His Son.

Quest of the Day

1. Read Leviticus Chapter 16.

2. Read Matthew Chapters 26 and 27.

3. Read Hebrews Chapters 9 and 10.

DAY 10: THE RESURRECTION OF SPOCK
BY NATHAN MARCHAND

Greater love has no one than this: that he lay down his life
for his friends.
John 15:13

Star Trek II: The Wrath of Khan is a classic for many
reasons, not the least of which is the iconic death of Spock.

The Enterprise has barely escaped a battle with the
tyrant Khan, but only because Spock ran into a radiation-
filled room to repair the ship's warp drive. Now Kirk sees his
best friend dying on the opposite side of a glass wall.

"The ship...out of danger?" Spock asks.

"Yes," replies Kirk, choking back tears.

"Don't grieve, Admiral. It is logical. The needs of the
many outweigh..."

"...the needs of the few..." Kirk finishes.

"...or the one. I have been, and always shall be, your
friend." With that, Spock places his hand on the glass,
sprawled in the Vulcan salute, and adds, "Live long and
prosper." Then his hand falls limp.

But Spock wasn't dead for long.

In *Star Trek III: The Search for Spock*, Kirk and
company learn that Spock transferred his *katra* (or soul) into
Dr. McCoy, and they need to go recover the Vulcan's body

and return to his homeworld to rejoin his body and soul. By the end of the film, after a harrowing adventure involving Klingons, an exploding planet, and the destruction of the Enterprise, Spock is resurrected.

This is one of many "resurrection" stories found throughout speculative fiction. Fans have come to accept, and even expect, them. Ultimately, their appeal stems from every person's need to know the greatest resurrection story of all—that of Jesus Christ.

Jesus, like Spock, sacrificed Himself to save others. He even went so far as to call His disciples His friends. "Greater love has no one than this; that he lay down his life for his friends. I no longer call you servants, because a servant does not know his master's business. Instead, I have called you friends, for everything I learned from my Father I have made known to you" (John 15:13, 15). Sounds eerily similar to Spock's dying words, doesn't it? Jesus didn't die for mankind's sins out of obligation—He did it because He loved mankind.

If death was the end of the story, it would be a noble yet tragic tale. But Jesus said, "...I lay down my life—only to take it up again" (John 10:17). Far from cheapening His sacrifice, it adds greater meaning to it. Death was not the end. Jesus came to give eternal life (John 10:10). Unlike Spock, who, despite being a long-living Vulcan, will one day die again, Jesus will never die again (1 Peter 3:18). So, while Spock's sacrifice was noble, it is but an echo of what Jesus did.

It is, as Spock would say, "fascinating" to think about.

Quest of the Day

1. Read Matthew 28, Mark 16, Luke 24, and John 20.
2. Is there anything that makes it difficult for you to believe in the resurrection? If so, write it down. If you know another Christian (in particular, a pastor), contact that person and talk it over with him or her.

DAY 11: THE RETURN OF THE KING OF KINGS
BY ERIC ANDERSON

And I heard a loud voice from the throne saying, "Look!
God's dwelling place is now among the people and He will
dwell with them."
Revelation 21:3

One day long ago, the first man made a choice that put himself over God. And we lost a great kingdom to our own selfishness. Now we all look forward to the final defeat of death and disease. The final destruction of sin. The return of Christ. Often we try to disguise this longing with stories of utopias. Or we doubt it because of stories about benevolent aliens that turn out to be planning to conquer us. Ultimately, the defeat of evil, sin, and death will come from Christ; not from us or any other society.

We know many things that will lead up to this:

- The Rapture, that is, the physical taking-away of Christians
- The seven-year tribulation and reign of the Anti-Christ
- Wars and rumors of wars
- Judgments upon mankind

We have many different ideas about the timing of all these things in relation to each other, but all these trials and events are pointing toward one thing: Christ coming back to establish His reign on the Earth. First, He'll have a reign of 1,000 years and eventually there will be a new heaven and a new earth.

Remember the joy at the end of *The Return of the King?* How Aragorn marries Arwen? As the kingdom of men is reuniting, you have this wedding attended by elves, dwarves, hobbits, and at least one wizard. They all come together to see the real king take back his throne after years of a fractured mankind.

Right now we have disunity. We have Catholics, Wesleyans, Presbyterians, Methodists, Baptists, Charismatic fellowships, Russian Orthodoxy, Greek Orthodoxy, and many other groups that argue over many different issues. We argue over free will and predestination; we argue over how we should be baptized; we argue over what kind of music we should use in our services.

Someday we will all gather around the throne of God to worship Him; all our languages and denominations and ethnicities; every individual from all of history who has committed themselves to the Lordship of Jesus Christ. We, who have accepted His forgiveness, will be there to take on new roles. We will lead a new society that will be focused on Christ as our Head. Styles of music won't matter. Our assumptions about the timing of events in the last days won't matter. Only our God's love for us and our love for Him will be the focus.

"Now the dwelling of God is with men, and he will live with them. They will be his people, and God himself will be with them and be their God. He will wipe every tear from their eyes. There will be no more death or mourning or crying or pain, for the old order of things has passed away." (Revelation 21:3-4)

I hope you will be joining us, that you have chosen Christ instead of trying to defeat sin on your own accord.

Quest of the Day

1. Read Mark 13 and Revelation 19.

2. Would you find these end-times events scary or exciting? Journal about that.

DAY 12: SIN ENTERED THE WORLD
BY NATHAN MARCHAND

Therefore, just as sin entered the world through one man,
and death through sin, and in this way death came to all
people, because all sinned....
Romans 5:12

The Magician's Nephew, the first (chronologically) of the *Chronicles of Narnia* books by C.S. Lewis, tells the story of Digory and his friend Polly, who travel to a ruined world called Charn via magic rings. There they meet a witch named Jadis, who had destroyed that world. She clings to the children as they use the rings to return to their world, where she wreaks havoc. Digory and Polly grab her and put on the rings, returning to the Woods Between the Worlds.

They jump into a pool, thinking it will return them to Charn, but instead are transported to a world in the process of being created by a great lion, who speaks animals, mythic creatures, and landscapes into existence. The lion's name is Aslan, and Jadis tries to spear him, but fails, so she flees. Aslan confronts Digory for bringing the evil Jadis to this new world, thereby introducing evil to it. He tells him he must atone for this by going to the mountains and bringing back a golden apple from a tree. He sends him off on a winged horse.

35

There, Digory finds the apple tree—and meets Jadis. She has eaten one of the apples and become immortal. She tempts him to eat one himself and join her in immortality, or steal one to take back to cure his sick mother. But Digory resists and goes back to Aslan with just one apple. Aslan is pleased and gives Digory an apple to take home to his mother.

While this book has a happy ending, the story it parallels didn't. Not yet.

God created the world and placed Adam and Eve in the Garden of Eden. The world was a paradise. They could eat of any tree except the Tree of the Knowledge of Good and Evil. Satan appeared in the form of a serpent and tempted Eve to eat of this tree, saying she would be like God. She did eat of it and shared that forbidden fruit with Adam.

Because of this sin—what theologians call Original Sin—evil was introduced to the world. Death became reality. Mankind would have to toil to eat. Adam and Eve lost their innocence and were ashamed of their nakedness. Since then, every human ever born has had a sinful nature. It's part of their "spiritual DNA," in a sense. They are bent toward doing wrong.

The Bible defines sin as missing the mark. In other words, not living up to God's standards of holiness. "All have sinned and fall short of the glory of God" (Romans 3:23). No matter what movies like *This is the End* may tell you, no amount of good deeds will earn you admittance into heaven. "The wages of sin is death" (Romans 6:23a). Not just physical death: spiritual death. In other words, an eternity in Hell. Simply put, Hell is eternal separation from God.

But there is still hope. We can have the happy ending seen in *The Magician's Nephew*. It involves meeting a real-life Aslan.

Quest of the Day

1. Read Genesis 3 and Romans 5:12-21.
2. What are your greatest vices? What sins have you committed recently? List them. You'll need this later.

DAY 13: SHAL'KEK NEM'RON!
BY ERIC ANDERSON

Therefore I urge you, brothers and sisters, in view of God's mercy, to offer your bodies as a living sacrifice, holy and pleasing to God—this is your true and proper act of worship.
Romans 12:1

I am an avid fan of the TV show *Stargate SG-1*. Very avid. (I even owned the full 10- season box set at one time.) The show's premise is a crew that explores new worlds through a device that can transport people between planets. Along the journey, you constantly see a race of beings called Jaffa, who are enslaved and used as warriors for a race called the Goa'uld.

At Barnes and Noble, I found a visual guide to the show. One of the cool things about this guide was a dictionary of Jaffa words/phrases. In this list was the phrase, "Kalach shal teck!" This phrase means, "Victory or death!" But this has a different meaning to the Jaffa. A more literal translation has the thought of one's soul returning home, either with or without the body. They often greeted each other with the phrase "Shal'kek nem'ron" or "I die free!"

This comes close to being a good slogan for Christianity, but misses the bar. Jesus told us:

"...anyone who does not take up his cross and follow me is not worthy of me. Whoever finds his life will lose it, and whoever loses his life for my sake will find it" (Matthew 10:38-39).

Like it is for the Jaffa, our way to victory is through death, or rather "death to self." In other words, living for God and denying our own selfishness. I have realized over the years that this has to happen daily, especially when there is an issue of sin.

Yet "Victory is death" is also close yet far away. Paul was torn between death to self and literal death.

"For to me, to live in Christ and to die is gain. If I am to go on living in the body, this will mean fruitful labor for me. Yet what shall I choose? I do not know! I am torn between the two: I desire to depart and be with Christ, which is better by far; but it is more necessary for you that I remain in the body" (Philippians 1:21-24).

I do not think Paul was thinking, "victory or death." In Romans 8 he tells us that we are "more than conquerors" and that "...in all things God works for the good of those who love Him...." Yet, he also quotes Psalm 44:22 in saying that for God's sake "...we face death all day long...." I think he meant, "Victory and death!" As Christians, we must face death in order to be victorious in Christ. Sometimes it is as simple as refusing our own sinful desires. Other times it is more external, such as Christians in certain parts of the world who could literally be killed and imprisoned for following Christ.

Kalak shal tek! Shal'kek nem'ron!

Quest of the Day

1. Read Luke 9:57-62 and Luke 14:25-33.
2. Have you ever taken time to count the cost of following Christ? Write down some thoughts on the cost of Christ. Things it has cost you or could cost you.
3. Is there a sin you need to die to?

DAY 14: REGENERATION
BY NATHAN MARCHAND

Therefore, if anyone is in Christ, he is a new creation; the old
has gone, the new has come!
2 Corinthians 5:17

"Behold! The miracle of the Time Lord!" announced
the Master while his seemingly-dead nemesis, the Doctor, laid
on the floor in the *Doctor Who* spoof, "The Curse of Fatal
Death." Within moments, the Doctor's face morphed before
his eyes and he stood, determined to thwart his enemies'
plans.

One of the fun things about being a Whovian (*Doctor
Who* fan) is debating who (no pun intended) was the best
Doctor. To date, 12 (or 13, depending on who you talk to)
actors have officially played the iconic Time Lord since 1963.
Four (or five, again depending on who you talk to) of them
have been on the insanely popular new series that began in
2005. This long succession was created back in the 1960s by
adding the concept of "regeneration" to the show's mythos.

What is regeneration?

When a Time Lord dies, his body releases a burst of
energy that reforms and revives him, thereby preserving his
life. In the process, his face changes and different aspects of
his personality are emphasized in each incarnation. For

example, the Ninth Doctor (the first to appear in the new series) was a melancholy, but fierce, man who wore a leather jacket. The Tenth Doctor looked younger, had a manic personality, often felt lonely, and wore a "geek chic" suit with converse shoes. The Eleventh Doctor was a quirky, even younger-looking man who loved wearing bowties. Yet they are all the same character.

While this allows the Doctor to cheat death, it has its limits. He can only do it 12 times (though the Doctor got around this). Many of his Companions are at first confused by his new appearance and personality. Regeneration also has unpleasant side effects. The Doctor must endure agonizing pain and illness each time it happens, and this often leaves him vulnerable to his enemies. But once the pain has subsided, he is a new man, ready to take on a universe of challenges.

Interestingly, "regeneration" is the word used by many old-time theologians to describe what happens when someone becomes a Christian. When he "confesses Jesus Christ as Lord" (Romans 10:9), God's Holy Spirit indwells him, wiping away his sins and renewing his mind (1 Cor. 6:11; Romans 12:1-2). He is the same person, yet he isn't. His personality is the same, but his attitude has changed. He doesn't want to live for himself, but to serve God and others. Once, he was bent toward sinning, but now he is bent toward righteous living. The Apostle Paul put it aptly when he said, "Therefore, if anyone is in Christ, he is a new creation; the old has gone, the new has come!" (2 Corinthians 5:17).

But, just as regeneration was unpleasant for the Doctor, so it is for the new Christian, spiritually-speaking. He will have to quit old sinful habits he enjoyed (illicit sex, drunkenness, etc.) His priorities will change. He will have to talk differently. In other words, his whole lifestyle will change, and it can be a difficult transition.

And much like the Doctor, this new Christian's old friends may be confused by these changes. They might even leave him. This will only make things harder. But the Doctor was always able to find new Companions to join him on his travels through time and space, and God will give the new Christian friends to join him on his spiritual journey.

Perhaps you're overdue for a regeneration.

Quest of the Day

1. Read Psalm 51.
2. Take the list you made on day 12 and prayerfully ask God to give you strength to resist temptation and also ask Him for forgiveness for each of your sins.

DAY 15: GUIDED PRAYER DAY – CONFESSION

This is the first of several days in the devotional dedicated exclusively to prayer. You may want to block out at least 30 minutes of your day in order to get everything in. Feel free to go longer, as the Spirit leads.

Today's focus will be on confession. You don't need a priest or anyone else to confess to. It's between you and God. However, if you'd like someone you trust to pray with you, invite him/her to join you.

1. If you have not accepted Jesus Christ as Savior, start with that. All you have to do is confess with your mouth and believe in your heart (Romans 10:9). However, if you'd like a scripted prayer, here's the Campus Crusade for Christ sinner's prayer: "Lord Jesus, I need You. Thank You for dying on the cross for my sins. I open the door of my life and receive You as my Savior and Lord. Thank You for forgiving my sins and giving me eternal life. Take control of the throne of my life. Make me the kind of person You want me to be."

2. If you still have that list of sins from day 12, confess them right now. God will not hold them against you. "He is faithful and just and will forgive us our sins and purify us from all unrighteousness" (1 John 1:9).

Name each sin one by one. If you forget any, make a blanket prayer. God will know what you're talking about.

3. God may bring people to mind who you've sinned against. Write their names down. Ask God for the strength, wisdom, and proper timing to confess those sins to them.

4. Praise God for His grace. You can thank Him in prayer or listen to some worship music and sing your praises.

5. Believe your sins are forgiven. If doubts creep into your mind, shut them out. They are most likely from the devil.

DAY 16: SPIDER-MAN AND THE PONG OF VENGEANCE BY ERIC ANDERSON

Bear with each other and forgive one another…Forgive
as the Lord forgave you.
Colossians 3:13

How often do you think about forgiveness? How often do you hear that word? We don't really stress it in our culture, do we? We encourage kids to forgive each other for little tantrums and we use the word once in a while. But do we, as a modern culture, really understand what it means? Do we use this gift and discipline as we should?

I don't think we do. When Peter asked Jesus how often we should forgive, he guessed "up to seven times." Jesus said, "Seventy times seven." After teaching His followers the "Lord's Prayer" (or the "Our Father," as the Catholics refer to it), he stated: "For, if you forgive men when they sin against you, your heavenly Father will also forgive you. But if you do not forgive men their sins, your heavenly father will not forgive your sins." (Matthew 6:14-15)

Jesus once told a parable about a King who was settling accounts with his servants. One man owed him 10,000 talents (money) and the king was going to sell the man, his family, and all he owned to settle it. But the man begged for patience. The King took pity on him and cancelled his debt (today that would be millions of dollars).

46

The servant went on his way and found a fellow servant who owed him a hundred denarii, or a few dollars. After choking the man, he threw him into prison for that small amount. After hearing about this, the King called the servant in. "I forgave you for millions and you couldn't forgive that other man for a few dollars?" He had the servant thrown not just into jail, but sent to a torturer to repay his millions.

Do you think Jesus thought forgiveness was important?

Think about Spider-Man and Sandman in *Spider-Man 3*. Spider-Man finds out that Sandman killed Uncle Ben. How difficult would that be? With the influence of the black costume, he sets out to destroy Sandman. During this he makes some other bad choices that hurt both Aunt May and Mary Jane. The vengeance that the symbiote encourages and feeds on only brings more pain to Peter Parker. What happens? First, Aunt May shows her horror at the idea of Spider-Man killing Sandman. Then, slowly, as his life unfurls, Peter starts to see the problems vengeance brings him. He has to seek partnership and forgiveness from his friend, Harry Osborn, (who had embraced vengeance toward Spider-Man) to save M.J. Eventually, he forgives Sandman. Then, after he speaks and acts out forgiveness, he and M.J. begin a long process of healing in their relationship. One act of forgiveness starts a process of healing (and more forgiveness) in multiple relationships.

In our day, we have a lot of misconceptions about forgiveness. Forgiving someone does not support or condone what was done. It does *not* mean you will trust him again. It simply means you won't hold it against him. You won't let his act (or failure to act) decide your view of him. The Greek words used for forgiveness refer to separating yourself completely for the act or of casting it away from you.

My pastor once related this to Pong. If we don't forgive, we keep a ball of pain going back and forth, again and again. This leads to more pain for everyone, and sometimes for people who are close to both parties. Forgiveness stops that ball. Yes, to heal you must stop the Pong of Vengeance.

Quest of the Day

1. Is there a person you need to write a letter to, expressing forgiveness for wronging you?

2. If someone hurt you and you can't communicate with them, pray out your forgiveness. Verbally say to God that you are forgiving him.

3. Is it hard to forgive someone? Write yourself a note saying, "I am forgiving…." I did this in college about a girl who had turned me down

romantically. Post it somewhere that you will see it regularly.

4.   Have you confessed a sin to God that shames you, but not forgiven yourself for it?

DAY 17: FIGHTING THE DARK HADOU
BY NATHAN MARCHAND

How can a young man keep his way pure? By living according
to Your word.
Psalm 119:9

Ryu is the greatest fighter in the *Street Fighter* video
game series. His most famous (and most imitated) move is a
blue fireball he forms by tapping into his *ki* and then
throwing it from his hands while exclaiming the move's
name: "Hadouken!" He has used this move to win martial
arts tournaments and defeat villains like the dictator M.
Bison, who plots to take over the world ("Of course!").

But an inner darkness plagues Ryu. Much like the
Force in *Star Wars*, there is a "dark side" to the *hadou*. This is
called the *Satsui no Hadou*, which when translated means,
"Surge of Murderous Intent." According to the Street Fighter
Wiki, this "is a form of *ki* that is rooted in the darker aspects
of natural human instinct (including the desire to survive,
trample, and impose over opposition) and, on a metaphysical
level, the natural occurrence and manifestation of loss,
decline, and destruction." It goes on to say, "To tap into [it], a
person must be so consumed with the desire to win, or else
possess such intense rage, that [he is] willing to kill."

This "dark *hadou*" consumed Akuma, who then
murdered his brother, Ryu's master, Gouken, with the power

50

it gave him. Akuma lost all his humanity and compassion, and now lives only to fight and kill.

Ryu also has this power within him, thanks to his great skill, but he refuses to tap into it, fearing it will corrupt him like it did Akuma. In *Street Fighter Alpha: The Animation*, Ryu nearly succumbs to the dark *hadou*, but is pulled from the brink by his best friend, Ken Masters. However, in several of the video games, there is a hypothetical version of Ryu who did embrace this dark power. This "Evil Ryu" is a murderous man with an insatiable appetite for violence, just like Akuma.

Thanks to the work of Christ, we have been given a new, purified nature. But our old, sinful nature was not wiped out. It constantly wars against us, refusing to die and demanding to sin. The Apostle Paul wrote about this struggle in Romans 7:19-20: "For I do not do the good I want to do, but the evil I do not want to do—this I keep on doing. Now if I do what I do not want to do, it is no longer I who do it, but it is sin living in me that does it."

The "old self," as Paul calls it, "was crucified with [Christ] so that the body of sin may be done away with" (Rom. 6:6) but, unfortunately, it is dying a slow death. We will never be free of sin until we reach Heaven. Until then, we will struggle with it.

But it isn't a hopeless fight. The psalmist wrote, "How can a young man keep his way pure? By living according to Your word. I have hidden Your word in my heart that I might not sin against You" (Psalm 119:9, 11). The more we obey God's commands, the more the "old self" dies, and the stronger we can resist sin. This is God's great desire for us for, once we are freed from sin, we can better serve Him and become the people He created us to be.

And that includes being the sort of warriors even Ryu would envy.

Quest of the Day

1. What temptations do you struggle with every day? What are some sins you want to be free of? Write them down. Pray for God to give you the strength to resist them and provide a means of escape.

2. If you face temptations in certain places or situations, try to avoid them today.

DAY 18: TRY ANOTHER GATE ADDRESS
BY ERIC ANDERSON

Do not be overcome by evil, but overcome evil with good.

Romans 12:21

I'm guessing you have been rejected at some point in your life. Maybe you were the last to be picked for a playground sport. Maybe you were turned down by someone you wanted to date. Maybe you were the one left out of the major office committee you wanted to be on, or they just didn't like any of your ideas and you were seen as little more than a drone for labor.

In the early seasons of *Stargate SG-1*, none of the friendly aliens like the Asgard, Knox, and Tok'ra would share advanced technology with the team. They acted as though Earth was a child. Now, in that case, they were probably correct. SG-1 still had a lot to learn about how it worked out there. General Hammond simply tried to be friends, even if they wouldn't share technology. One group, however, went behind his back, stealing technology. After being approached about this by several of the more technologically-advanced races, Col. O'Neil went undercover and managed to get close enough to alert Stargate Command and the allies as to the off-world location of this group. Eventually, the Asgard started sharing technology with the SGC. And they gained some in battles with the evil Goa'uld. But they did not steal from those who rejected them.

So how do we respond to rejection? "Then Peter came to Jesus and asked, 'Lord, how many times shall I forgive my brother when he sins against me? Up to seven times?' Jesus answered, 'I tell you, not seven times, but seventy times seven times'" (Mathew 18:21-22).

Some forms of rejection are sin, but some are not. Most situations of romantic rejection are not sin (although sin may have played other roles in such situations). But forgiveness is still needed. Any time someone hurts you, forgiveness is needed. But sometimes that hurt comes from a choice that is not sinful. Still, forgive them.

After forgiving, don't expect anyone *except* Jesus to fulfill you.

Catholic priest and professor Henri Nouwen writes, "There is much mental suffering in our world. But some of it is suffering for the wrong reason because it is born out of the false expectation that we are called to take each other's loneliness away. When our loneliness drives us away from ourselves into the arms of our companions in life, we are, in fact, driving ourselves into excruciating relationships, tiring friendships, and suffocating embraces."[1]

---

[1] Henri J. M. Nowen *Reaching Out* Pages 29/30 Image Books/Double Day

The Psalmist offers an alternative: "Many are asking, 'Who can show us any good?' Let the light of your face shine upon us, O Lord. You have filled my heart with greater joy than when their grain and new wine abound. I will lie down and sleep in peace, for you alone, O Lord, make me dwell in safety" (Psalm 4:6-8).

Jesus will take care of you, no matter who has turned you down. He doesn't reject people, and He always listens. He is not a genie. He won't give you everything you want. But He is GOD and He will fill your desires with good things. The Psalmist recognizes that God is his source and that God will do more for him than provisions from others. Everyone around him is looking horizontally and not vertically. They want and expect humans to provide, but the Psalmist says, "…for you alone, O Lord, make me dwell in safety."

Are you trusting God today, or looking for hope from man?

Quest of the Day

1. Read Gen. 37 and Gen. 45.
2. How has a rejection helped you learn something important? How has one opened a door that included God doing some amazing things in your life?

DAY 19: IN REMEMBRANCE OF CAPTAIN AMERICA
BY NATHAN MARCHAND

The Lord Jesus, on the night he was betrayed, took bread, and when he had given thanks, He broke it and said, "This is my body, which is broken for you; do this in remembrance of me." In the same way, after supper He took the cup, saying, "This cup is the new covenant in my blood; do this in remembrance of me."
1 Corinthians 11:23b-25

In the Marvel Universe, both in comics and in the movies, Captain America is considered to be one of the first superheroes. If not the first, he's the one most of the others look up to as an example of how to be a hero. Not because he's the most powerful, but because he's moral, dedicated, and patriotic.

In the film, *Captain America: The First Avenger*, after Cap (as his friends call him) seemingly died crashing a plane, carrying a weapon that could destroy New York City, he became a legend. Everyone knew him by name. Little boys painted trashcan lids like his iconic shield and ran around in the streets. Agent Coulson told Cap in *The Avengers* that he collected vintage baseball cards featuring him.

When Cap died after the events of *Civil War* comic series in the mid-2000s, he appeared to be buried in Arlington Cemetery with a huge memorial (he was actually laid to rest at sea). Most of the Marvel heroes shared stories about Cap or why they admired him. The world wasn't the same without him.

Communion, one of the oldest practices in Christianity, is about remembrance. Much like Cap was memorialized, Christians are commanded to remember Jesus Christ and His sacrifice on the cross. Jesus told His disciples at the Last Supper that He was instituting a new covenant, one made in His own blood. The bread symbolized His body, which "was pierced for our transgressions" (Isa. 53:5), and the wine represented His blood.

When the church was established after His ascension, communion was a large feast held by churches to celebrate this new covenant and remember Jesus' holy work. Nowadays, churches practice communion in different ways, ranging from dispersing crackers and small cups of grape juice to the congregation, to full-fledged dinners. However, the purpose remains the same: remembering the life, death, and resurrection of Jesus Christ.

It reminds me of a picture I saw on the Internet that featured Jesus talking with Spider-Man, Hulk, and Captain America. The superheroes are listening to Him intently, and the voice bubble above Jesus' head says, "And that's how I saved the world!"

Quest of the Day

1. Read 1 Corinthians 11:17-33.

2. Find out the next time your church is having Communion. Plan to attend and participate.

3. Or, if you prefer, you can have communion by yourself with your own grape juice and bread. I recommend reading the above Bible passage and saying a short prayer.

DAY 20: THE TONGUE AND WATER CRYSTALS
BY ERIC ANDERSON

Whoever conceals hatred with lying lips and spreads slander
is a fool.
Proverbs 10:18

Water is impacted by what you say. Strange thought, huh? Water responds to sounds?

A Japanese scientist named Dr. Masaru Emoto wanted to find out if this was true. So, he started experimenting with it in 1994. He thought that ice might have crystals similar to that of snow. When he froze the water and put it under a microscope, he did indeed find crystals. In fact, they were three-dimensional crystals.

After he realized he could do this, he started doing something more with the idea. He got some distilled water and spoke to it. Sometimes he would say nice things like, "I love you, water," or, "You are beautiful, water." Then he started insulting it with phrases like, "I hate you, water," or, "You are ugly, water." Somehow, and quite puzzlingly, the water responded. After speaking good things to the water, the crystals were beautiful, symmetrical, and absolutely amazing to look at. Then there were the crystals formed after being insulted. These were ugly and warped.

Now, this experiment sounds weird and strange, but you can go to his website at www.masaru-emoto.net. I first heard about this from a Hong Kong preacher on GodTV and then we talked about this during my discipleship training in Slovakia.

Here is the thing about this. www.Chemistry.about.com says the human body has anywhere from 50-75% of its make-up in *water*. Yeah. Let that sink in a little. *The molecule that makes up 70% of your body responds to encouraging words and discouraging words differently.*

James, the brother of Jesus, wrote about the issue of the tongue: "All kinds of animals, birds, reptiles and creatures of the sea are being tamed and have been tamed by man, but no man can tame the tongue. It is a restless evil, full of deadly poison. With the tongue we praise the Lord and Father, and with it we curse men, who have been made in God's likeness. Out of the same mouth come praise and cursing. My brothers this should not be." (James 3:7-10)

He also compared the tongue to a ship's rudder and the bit in the mouth of a horse. With a small item, you change the focus or the course of larger entities. Such is true of your words. The way you speak affects you and the people around you. Proverbs has some advice about this:

"From the fruit of his lips a man enjoys good things, and but the unfaithful have a craving for violence" (Proverbs 13:2).

"He who guards his lips guards his life, but he who speaks rashly will come to ruin" (Proverbs 13:3).

Now, Doctor Emoto is not a Christian. He was not trying to prove anything about the Bible, but what he observed supports the Bible's warning that the way you speak affects many things and, most of all, it affects the people around you.

There are two applications here. Be respectful in how you speak to others. Don't be a jerk. Playful banter can be fun, but know the difference between a little light teasing and hurting someone. Sometimes we think we know the difference, but we are not living like it. Next, be careful how you speak about yourself. You are a creation of God. You are loved and appreciated by Him. Watch what you say about yourself, because it will affect you.

Quest of the Day

1. Read Galatians 5:22.
2. How can you allow these principals to guide your speech?
3. Call a friend or pull him/her aside and tell him/her how he/she has helped you. Encourage him/her.

DAY 21: MOTHRA'S SONG
BY NATHAN MARCHAND

Do not be anxious about anything, but in everything, by
prayer and petition, with thanksgiving, present your requests
to God.
Philippians 4:6

If you grew up watching Godzilla movies, you
probably ran around singing, "Mosura ya, Mosura!" This was
the opening line of a song sung by the tiny (as in six inches
tall) twin priestesses of Mothra, the benevolent and beautiful
insect monster. Whenever danger struck, these girls would
sing this song to petition Mothra to intervene. Often, they
themselves would get into trouble and call Mothra for help
using this song.

What's interesting is sometimes Mothra came
immediately, sometimes she didn't. In the original *Godzilla vs.
Mothra*, when the characters visited Mothra's island to petition
her to stop Godzilla's rampage, the big bug refused to at first,
since the Japanese had taken one of her eggs. The characters
had to appeal to Mothra's better nature to convince her to
help them. Other times, like in *Godzilla and Mothra: The Battle
for Earth*, she acts quickly in response to the song of her
priestesses.

This exotic-sounding ditty was originally written in Malay and later rewritten in Japanese, but if you ever wondered what the lyrics really were, here's a translation:

Mothra, O Mothra
If we were to call for help
Over time
Over sea
Like a wave you'd come
Our guardian angel

Mothra, O Mothra
Of forgotten kindness
And ruined spirits
We pray for people's spirit as we sing
This song of love

Almost sounds like a psalm, doesn't it? It could even be called a prayer.

If even fictional pint-sized priestess can pray to a massive mystical moth, how much more we should be honored and encouraged to pray to the God of the Universe!

Prayer is a discipline that is shrouded in mystery. Jesus said, "Your Father knows what you need before you ask Him" (Matt. 6:8), yet He still wants us to petition Him with our requests. Eric's mother says she once prayed for God to help her open a pickle jar that was stuck, and, after looking away from it briefly, found it opened. Yet other people have prayed for the physical healing of an ailing family member or friend, but that person never recovers. Or the opposite has happened and the "big" request is answered and the "little" one isn't.

However, the Apostle John offers this reassurance: "This is the confidence we have in approaching God: that if we ask anything according to His will, He hears us. And if we know that He hears us—whatever we ask—we know that we have what we asked of Him" (1 John 5:14-15).

Prayer is ultimately about communicating with God. It can be done by simply talking to Him. Or it can be done creatively. Like Mothra's twin priestesses, the psalmist sang his prayers to his God. If you're a writer, you could keep a prayer journal or write poetic prayers. However you do it, remember to "pray continually" (1 Thes. 5:17).

In other words, pray about everything!

Quest of the Day

1. Read Psalm 34 and Matthew 6:5-15.
2. Write a list of prayer requests for yourself and others. Make effort to pray about them daily, believing God will answer.

DAY 22: STEPPING AWAY
BY ERIC ANDERSON

"Go, assemble all the Jews who are found in Susa, and fast
for me; do not eat or drink for three days, night or day. I and
my maidens also will fast in the same way. And thus I will go
in to the king, which is not according to the law; and if I
perish, I perish."
Esther 4:16

"I'm leaving the team."

J'onn J'onzz, the Martian Manhunter, shocked the
ears of Wonder Woman, Green Arrow, and others when he
said this in the DC Animated series *Justice League Unlimited*.
J'onn had been in the Watchtower for nearly two years. The
only contacts he had were the Leaguers and their support
staff. He had lost touch with humanity.

We need to recharge and reconnect with God
sometimes. A common practice for this is fasting. The idea of
fasting is that you give up sometime important to you, even
important for your survival, for the purpose of saying, "My
source is God." You do this to form a deeper connection.

Jesus fasted for forty days right before He started His
ministry. Esther had the Israelites fast for three days as part
of a plan to save the Jews from genocide. In Jesus' teachings,
He did not command us to fast, but He expected it.

In Mathew 6:16-18, He says, "When you fast, do not
look somber as the hypocrites do, for they disfigure their

faces to show men that they are fasting. I tell you the truth; they have received their reward in full. But when you fast, put oil on your head and wash your face, so that it will not be obvious to men that you are fasting, but only to your Father, who is unseen; and your Father who sees what is done in secret will reward you."

He told us "when" we fast, not "if" we fast. In that day, fasting was a normal way of life. For some it was as common as going to the movies is for many Americans. Here are a few tips for fasting from food:

1. Always connect it with prayer. They go hand in hand.

2. If you have not fasted from food before, start with a one-day fast or even just a single-meal fast. Don't jump to multi-day fasting immediately.

3. Don't drink acidic liquids while fasting from food, as it will be hard on your stomach.

I remember several times when God called me to fast from specific items, but it wasn't always food. Several times I have had the call to fast from gaming, particularly table-top gaming. During one season of Lent, I even went so far as to try not to think about games or look at them in stores. I found that fasting from games helped me keep them in perspective. It became less common for me to daydream about them and gave me space to think about other things.

I also remember two particular times when I found victory through fasting. One day at work I felt a little odd. Something just didn't feel right spiritually, and I couldn't put a finger on it. I think my church was doing a day of prayer and fasting, but it didn't feel like it was connected with that. I just had a feeling of spiritual oppression, like something pushing on me or that something dangerous was going on somewhere. During lunch I fasted and prayed, and continued praying when back at work, trying to figure out what was going on. To this day, I am not totally sure what was going on, but after fasting and praying the oppression left me. Another time I was feeling lonely, but I could tell that the loneliness was being pushed by the enemy. The enemy was trying to get me to blur the boundaries in a friendship with a girl. I knew I couldn't let that happen. So, I fasted from breakfast and prayed. Soon other things came to my mind, and the loneliness left me.

Take a lesson from the Martian Manhunter, and recognize your need to reconnect.

Quest of the Day

1. Read the book of Esther. How did fasting play a role in saving the Jews?

2. Plan and commit to a fast. Fast a meal or a day. Pray for the city you live in as you fast.

DAY 23: MIRACLE MAX, WESTLEY, AND WORSHIP BY NATHAN MARCHAND

Yet a time is coming and has now come when the true worshippers will worship the Father in spirit and in truth, for they are the kind of worshippers the Father seeks. God is spirit, and His worshippers must worship in spirit and in truth.
John 4:23-24

One of the most memorable characters from *The Princess Bride* is Miracle Max, a grumpy old medicine man. Inigo and Fezzik go to him to get a potion to revive Westley—who has been "mostly dead"—so they can go rescue Buttercup. But Max refuses to help, even when Westley whispers that his reason for wanting to live is "true love." Max's wife, Valerie, then comes in and chastises her husband for refusing to help, explaining to the men that Max once worked for the villainous Humperdink but was fired. This destroyed his confidence.

"Get back, witch!" Max cries.

Valerie replies, "I'm not a witch. I'm your wife. But after what you just said, I'm not even sure I want to be that anymore."

Westley, on the other hand, hadn't let the tragedies of his life make him bitter and angry. Though he feared Buttercup had forgotten him, once he learned the truth, he forgave her and continued to love her. In other words, love was still a part of his lifestyle. It permeated every part of him, affected everything he did. He adored her. He was even willing to die for her.

Worship is the same way. It's more than just singing songs at church on a Sunday morning. It's a lifestyle. The Apostle Paul said in Colossians 3:17, "Whatever you do, whether in word or deed, do it all in the name of the Lord Jesus, giving thanks to God the Father through Him." That means everything a Christian does, from the mundane to the spectacular, should be worship. It's not just a Sunday morning thing. It's an attitude.

Worship includes reverence, awe, and thankfulness. It reminds us Christians that we serve a God far bigger than us, and we owe Him due praise. But we can praise Him with more than our voices. God is praised when we use the spiritual gifts He gave us to serve and admonish others. He also gave us talents and abilities, and if they're used in a similar manner, He is pleased. But we Christians must be humble enough to give Him the glory for everything we do. It's not about us—it's about Him.

Are you Westley or Miracle Max?

Quest of the Day

1. If you have a CD with worship music on it, listen to it in your room, at work, or in your car. If you can sing without disturbing anyone, do so.

2. Ask your pastor if there is any volunteer work you can do at your church. If so, commit to do it.

DAY 24: KNOWING IS HALF THE BATTLE!
BY ERIC ANDERSON

All scripture is God-breathed and is useful for teaching,
rebuking, correcting and training in righteousness, so that the
servant of God may be thoroughly equipped for every good
work.
1 Timothy 3:16

"Yo Joe!" started ringing in the hearts of American
kids in 1983. G.I. Joe was fighting the evil terrorist
organization Cobra, and all the kids wanted in on the action.
Sunbow Productions decided to use this for some good, and
started airing PSAs about topics ranging from not playing in
construction zones, to surviving a fire, to dealing with
bullying. They always included normal kids interacting with
members of the G.I. Joe team. They always ended with the
simple phrase, "Knowing is half the battle."

Isn't that a true statement? You cannot act on what
you do not know, but you cannot know what you do not
learn. We know that study was a major part of life for many
of our favorite Bible characters. Moses must have had quite
an education growing up in the Egyptian royal family, and he
had some training when he was taken in by his father-in-law,
Jethro. Samuel the prophet studied under Eli the high priest.
Daniel went through extensive training before his position in

the government. Jesus "grew in stature and in favor with God and men" (Luke 2:52).

The Psalmist writes: "How can a young man keep his way pure? By living according to your word. I seek you with all my heart; do not let me stray from your commands. I have hidden your word in my heart that I might not sin against you. Praise be to you, O Lord; teach me your decrees. With my lips I recount all the laws that come from your mouth. I rejoice in following your statutes as one rejoices in great riches. I meditate on your precepts and consider your ways. I delight in your decrees; I will not neglect your word" (Psalm 119:9-16).

Jesus chose twelve disciples to follow Him. They learned His ways by living with Him and travelling with Him. That is what a disciple does. They study their master's teachings, his lifestyle. They ask him questions and they watch him. Every little detail is important.

Think about it this way: How can you play a table-top game if you don't know all the rules? It doesn't matter if it is a RPG, a Euro game such as Settlers of Catan, or a big box game; you have to know the rules to play. If I didn't know that a plane can take out any target in the board game "Attack!", I would not be able to use my planes well. If I didn't know that in Settlers of Catan I can trade four of any resource for one of another resource, I might end up having a lot of things stolen by the robber on a roll of seven. To be effective, you must know the rules.

So, what are some study tips for life?

1. **Study your Bible.** Memorize scripture, but go beyond that. Learn how different passages relate to each other. Look for the context of the verse you are reading.

2. **Study with others.** Attend church regularly. Join a small group or a Bible study. Tell others your questions about life and the Bible.

3. **Study others.** Watch those around you closely and compare their lifestyle with scripture. Notice good patterns that you can add to your life.

4. **Study literature.** Read books about spiritual growth or use devotionals. Appendix A is a list of resources that I have found to be useful and thought-provoking.

"Knowing is half the battle." Internalizing the Word of God is the first step to applying it, but only the first step of a large journey. As you build a good pattern of studying the Word of God, you need to be applying it. A pastor at my church once told the story of a businessman in our congregation. He started reading the book of Proverbs in the Old Testament. As he started applying what he was reading to his business, his business grew.

Quest of the Day

1. Read Psalm 119:97-112.

2. How is the Word of God linked with difficult times in this passage?

3. Read James 1:22-25.

4. Write down a memory of how the Word of God helped you deal with something. If you can't remember one, start studying and applying. You'll have one soon enough.

DAY 25: THE DARK KNIGHT CONFESSES
BY NATHAN MARCHAND

He who conceals his sins does not prosper, but whoever
confesses and renounces them finds mercy.
Proverbs 28:13

The ending of *The Dark Knight* left people stunned.
Batman took the blame for Harvey Dent/Two-Face's killings
in order to "prove" that Joker couldn't corrupt the best of
them. While Batman was heroic, even Christ-like, in taking
Harvey's sins upon himself, this "victory" was based on a lie.
Could it even be called a victory?

Not only that, but Alfred, Bruce Wayne's butler,
received a letter from Bruce's love interest, Rachel, that said
she loved Harvey Dent and that she couldn't be with Bruce
so long as he was Batman. Unfortunately, Rachel died before
Alfred could give Bruce the letter, and Bruce believed Rachel
was waiting for him. So, Alfred burned the letter, keeping the
truth to himself.

But even lies with the best of intentions have a way of
eating away at the liars, as *The Dark Knight Rises* shows. Eight
years later, Gotham is experiencing an unprecedented peace,
thanks to legislation made in Harvey's honor. But
Commissioner Gordon can no longer live with the secret, and
has prepared a confessional speech. Bruce has quit being

Batman, still mourning Rachel because he believes he lost the love of his life. Finally, everything breaks. Alfred tells Bruce the truth. Gordon's speech is stolen by Bane and read on TV to all of Gotham, which forces Gordon to come clean with officer John Blake.

Initially, the consequences of these confessions are grave. Gotham is thrown into chaos by Bane. Bruce fires Alfred. But eventually the truth sets them free.

There's an old saying that goes, "Confession is good for the soul." Keeping our sins a secret is a terrible burden. It's lonely suffering. It puts walls between us and God. It damages our relationships with others. But when we confess them, we release ourselves of this burden. We can accept God's forgiveness. Our friends and family can bear our burdens with us (Gal. 6:2). It frees us from the bondage of our sins.

No wonder Catholic priests set up booths for parishioners to confess their sins.

This is a frightening prospect. We fear that people— even other Christians—will reject us because of our sins. Rest assured that such "Christians" are nothing but modern-day Pharisees. They've forgotten that "all have sinned and fallen short of the glory of God" (Rom. 3:23). That includes them. They're in the same boat as everyone else. Thankfully, many still remember this, and they will do what they can to help you.

More importantly, there is no sin beyond God's grace. God knows what you've done, even if you did it in secret, so there's no point in trying to hide it from Him. Even so, He won't hold it against you. 1 John 1:9 says, "If we confess our sins, He is faithful and just and will forgive us our sins and purify us from all unrighteousness."

So, confess your sins, and you will rise like the Dark Knight because God will lift you up.

Quest of the Day

1. Pray for God to reveal any unconfessed sins to you. If He brings some to mind, ask for forgiveness.

2. If God brings to mind any people you need to reconcile with, contact at least one of them and apologize to them.

DAY 26: PROFESSOR X, MAGNETO, AND SOLITUDE
BY ERIC ANDERSON

But Jesus often withdrew to lonely places and prayed.
Luke 5:16

We live in a busy society. There are always more people to talk to, more places to go, and more tasks to complete. Is that any different than previous generations? I am tempted to say "definitely." However, I think the difference isn't in that. It is in the abundance of noise and distractions. Think about it. Before radio and television, stillness was easier to find. Now we have gone beyond that to the Internet, iPads, video games, etc. Yet many are still feel alone.

Jesus often went to places to be alone. He sought out solitude. The night before he chose his twelve disciples, He spent time in a lonely place, praying. The Gospels are full of instances when He sought out solitude, including the night before He was crucified. If Jesus, who healed lepers and taught infinite truth, needed that, why do we assume we do not? Why didn't Jesus just "heal" Himself when He was stressed, then move on and do more healing and teaching?

This starts with a physical location. Do you have a place to go? Superman has the Fortress of Solitude. Batman has the Batcave. Where is your place? Maybe, if you have a roommate or live in a small house, you need to pick a time instead of a place. Either way, locate an area where you can be alone, away from everything. It doesn't have to be fully silent, just a place where you can contemplate, study, and listen to God. You don't need a mansion, just a room or some space outside.

I find the difference between Professor Xavier and Magneto quite interesting. Magneto acts out of his hatred toward oppressors. Xavier acts out of an inner compassion and an inner peace.

"In your anger do not sin; when you are on your beds, search your hearts and be silent" (Psalm 4:4).

But, this isn't about a physical place. You need to transform from loneliness to solitude. You need to create a heart of solitude to take with you anywhere you go. You see, people are often lonely in the middle of meetings, while greeting friends, or even when surrounded by crowds at concerts. Isn't that why Professor Xavier does so well? He controls himself with solitude instead of trying to gain power over the X-Men or any others.

So, how do you do that? Start by facing the loneliness. Stop trying to get rid of it and accept it. I think Jesus was fully aware of the fact that there was no one like Him on Earth. Did He get frustrated with His disciples? *All the time*. But He knew His place and their place in the story of faith. He didn't expect them to carry His burden. Xavier could use his telepathic abilities to make people be with him when he is lonely, but he doesn't.

Next, listen. "Though silence sometimes involves the absence of speech, it always involves the act of listening."[2] Read your Bible. Watch the people around you. Give God opportunities for speaking to you.

Finally, slow down. Don't rush all the time. Take the time to notice and enjoy your surroundings. Again, Professor X doesn't rush into battles. He takes time to figure out what is going on because his anger isn't what fuels him, unlike Magneto. He is always calm in his decisions and movements.

Let me leave you with a story from a village in Germany. Herrnut is a small place. Not much to see, except for some paper stars they sell as Christmas decorations. In German its name means to "abide under the Lord's watch." In the 1700s, the town, full of people who had sought refuge and religious safety on the land of Count Zinzendorf, had one service of prayer, confession, and forgiveness. This led to a 24-hour prayer chain in one room that lasted for 100 years. As the people of Herrnhut kept this practice of solitude, they started sending out missionaries. These missionaries went to China, the Americas, Morocco, and South Africa. The man

---

[2] Richard J. Foster "Celebration of Discipline" Page 98 Family Christian Press

who first started to translate the Bible into a Chinese dialect came from there, and is buried there. Because of this practice of solitude, developed and kept continually by an entire town, thousands of people and countless ethnic groups heard the Gospel.

If you take time for God and yourself, what could you accomplish with the rest of your time?

Quest of the Day

Spend five to 20 minutes alone. Just enjoy your atmosphere and be available for God to speak.

DAY 27: GUIDED PRAYER: PRAYING FOR CHURCH LEADERS

Today, we are praying for the church leaders; the men and women who spend countless hours and energy studying, setting up rooms, planning, preaching, leading worship, and counseling.

1. Begin with worship. Read a Psalm out loud. You may want to put worship music on in the background.

2. Pray for leaders who have impacted your relationship with Christ. The person who led you to Christ. A key small group leader or Sunday school leader. Thank God for their commitment and initiation.

3. Next, pray for the pastors and elders of your current church. Pray for wisdom, sanity, clarity of mind, good health, and joy. Pray that they would stay strong in the middle of temptation and be wise with finances.

4. Next, pray for other churches in your city. Every church that is following Jesus is a different expression of the Kingdom of God. Pray that they would be successful in pointing people toward Jesus, that they would be united together

and not bicker, and that they would be open to the leading of the Holy Spirit.

5. Pray for protection from the enemy for the pastors in your town.

6. Pray for the counseling pastors and Christian counselors in your city, that they would know how to help people, that people would be receptive to wise counsel.

7. Pray for leaders of Christian organizations. Organizations like Campus Crusade for Christ, Youth for Christ, Love Inc., A Christian Ministry in the National Parks, etc. Pray for the organizations by name. Pray that they would experience Christ, that they would be wise with finances, and that people would cooperate with them.

8. Pray for provision for the calling of God on the pastors of your city or area. Pray for both financial provision and volunteers to assist with the work.

9. Thank God for what He has already done in your church, and what He will do in the future.

10. Send a note of encouragement or thanksgiving to one of your pastors. Feel free to do this online or on paper.

DAY 28: FROM JERK TO HERO
BY NATHAN MARCHAND

Do nothing out of selfish ambition or vain conceit, but in
humility consider others better than yourselves.
Philippians 2:3

Tony Stark (aka Iron Man) was a man who had it all.
He was the smartest guy in the room wherever he went. He
was, as Johnny Storm said in the *Fantastic Four* movie, "richer
than God." He was so charming that he could even seduce
spiteful female reporters, as the first *Iron Man* film showed.
And he did it all with no regard for who he might hurt in the
process. All that mattered was his ambition.

That is, until he went to the front lines to
demonstrate his newest toy for the military. In an instant, he
was mortally wounded. Captured by the enemy, his life was
saved by a fellow prisoner, a doctor, who attached a device to
his chest that acted as a pacemaker for his damaged heart.
Determined to escape, Tony forged a high-tech suit of armor
so he could fight his captors. His friend the doctor sacrificed
his life to help Tony. He learned that if he removed the
pacemaker, he would die. Tony realized he needed to do
more with his life than make money and charm the ladies.
Since then, he built numerous armors to battle evil as the
superhero Iron Man.

Sounds a lot like the Apostle Paul, doesn't it? In the book of Acts, Paul, who was then named Saul, first appeared as a great persecutor of the church. He was present at the stoning of Stephen, the first Christian martyr (Acts 8:1). He was a Pharisee, a member of the Jewish religious elite. In Philippians 3:5-6, Paul wrote that he was "a Hebrew of Hebrews" and regarding "legalistic righteousness" he was "faultless."

But that all changed when he met Jesus Christ on the road to Damascus (Acts 9). Then he saw the face of the One he was persecuting. This experience blinded him. It wasn't until he met other Christians who, through prayer, restored his sight that he changed. Ironically, God chose him to proclaim the Gospel to the Gentiles. Through Paul, the Gospel reached as far as Gaul (Spain) and two-thirds of the New Testament was written.

Paul knew the pointlessness of selfish ambition. He even thought he was serving God when he oversaw the persecution of Christians as a Pharisee. We were much the same in our former lives until we, too, came to Christ. Even now, though, we must battle against selfishness. Going back to Iron Man, Tony Stark still had to resist the urge to show off and look out only for himself, even after becoming a hero. But God is always willing to forgive, as Paul learned.

It's time to burn selfish ambition and start living like a hero. But you don't have to do it alone. Iron Man joined the Avengers. You have fellow Christians. Joining a team is a great way to live unselfishly.

Quest of the Day

1. Write down your goals, dreams, and aspirations. If any of them are ungodly, discard them. If God reveals that your motivations are selfish for seeking the rest, ask for forgiveness.

2. Make a game plan for accomplishing your goals. You may want to meet with a mentor to help you figure that out.

DAY 29: THE ROUND TABLE VS. THE DESTINY BY ERIC ANDERSON

Now you are the body of Christ, and each one of you is a part
of it.
1 Corinthians 12:27

Stargate SG-1 spawned two spinoff series. One was *Stargate: Atlantis.* I thoroughly enjoyed it and was upset when it was cancelled. The other one, *Stargate Universe,* wasn't as good. It had a great premise and some intriguing ideas, but it could be described as this: a lot of arguing and a little bit of space travel. The crew of the Destiny had no teamwork or respect for each other. Sure, they were in a tight, difficult situation. But instead of cooperating and sharing, they fought. The soldiers and the scientists did not trust each other. The focus of the show was not on them overcoming disagreements, but on them disagreeing. The characters were more focused on their own goals than creating goals together. This made the show far less "re-watchable."

Now here's the thing: we act this way in the Christian community all the time. One elder wants to pursue this opportunity; another fights for that opportunity. One person wants rock and roll worship; another wants an organ and a choir.

James describes it as follows in James 4:1-3: "What causes fights and quarrels among you? Don't they come from your desires that battle within you? You want something but don't get it. You kill and covet, but you cannot have what you want. You quarrel and fight. You do not have because you do not ask. When you ask, you do not receive because you ask with wrong motives, that you may spend what you get on your pleasures."

So, how did Jesus want us to be? After praying for the disciples, He prayed for *us*. That's right. Jesus prayed for you and for me and for us together. Here is what He asked for:

"My prayer is not for them alone. I pray also for those who will believe in me through their message, that all of them may be one, Father, just as you are in me and I am in you. May they also be in us so that the world may believe that you have sent me. I have given them the glory that you gave me, that they may be one as we are one: I in them and you in me. May they be brought to complete unity to let the world know that you sent me and have loved them even as you have loved me" (John 17:20-23).

Do you see a difference here? Jesus wanted us to be united in Him to bring His love into the world. Instead, we argue over musical styling, service times, or whether to dunk someone in baptism or to sprinkle them. We argue over what translation of the Bible to use (even though the Bible was not written in English and so it doesn't matter which English version we use). *Jesus doesn't want this!* He wants unity. He wants us to work together and help each other. To build bridges, not walls.

In his court, King Arthur did something contrary to culture and precedent. He created a round table. Then he had his knights sit together. They all an idea about whatever matters they discussed. Now, King Arthur was still the decision-maker, but he accepted the input and opinions of every member of his team. I'm sure they argued from time to time. It is hard to agree together. Arguing is not always a bad thing, but do we see each other on the same level? Do we respect each other when we disagree? Do we trust each other?

I remember something like this while I was serving overseas. I come from a Wesleyan background and roomed with a Presbyterian teammate. We worked with Catholics, a couple with no denominational background, and Charismatics. All while attending a Nazarene Church. We were able to support the full-time missionaries by helping to teach English and put on a weekly refugee program for children. We disagreed sometimes, but we cooperated. We all grew up a little bit those three months. We fasted together, read the Bible together, prayed together and worshiped together. And we all still talk to this day.

Quest of the Day

1. Read 1 Corinthians 12:12-27.

2. Call a church or two that you do not attend and ask for prayer requests. I strongly recommend churches that are not in your church's denomination. Then pray for them regularly for a week.

DAY 30: FANTASTIC GIFTS
BY ERIC ANDERSON

Now to each one the manifestation of the Spirit is given for
the common good.
1 Corinthians 12:7

Has anyone ever asked you what superpower you
wish you had? I would love to be able to teleport or fly.
Would you want to heal people? Maybe you wish you had
pyrokinesis or technokinesis.

The Fantastic Four lived in a world that needed such
people desperately. They didn't even know how badly until
they got their powers. They were on a space mission when
some cosmic radiation bombarded them. Sue Storm gained
the ability to turn invisible and create force fields. Her
brother, Johnny Storm, gained the ability to engulf himself in
flames and fly. Reed Richards gained the ability to stretch his
body around in ridiculous ways. The one with the biggest
transformation, Ben Grimm, became a super-strong stone
goliath.

Have you been through a transformation like that? If
you have accepted Christ, you have. As soon as you did, the
Holy Spirit started flowing through you. This brought "gifts"
with it, but let's call them what they are...superpowers! You
were empowered and sustained by the Holy Spirit, not by

your desires (although the Holy Spirit does change your desires over time).

"Now to each one the manifestation of the Spirit is given for the common good. To one there is given through the Spirit the message of wisdom, to another the message of knowledge by means of the same Spirit, to another faith by the same Spirit, to another gifts of healing by that one Spirit, to another miraculous powers, to another prophecy, to another distinguishing between spirits, to another speaking in different kinds of tongues, and to still another the interpretation of the tongues. All these are the work of one and the same Spirit, and he gives them to each one, just as he determines" (1 Corinthians 12:7-11).

These gifts are not given to you so you can showboat or make money. They were given "for the common good." Notice how this works out? One person receives a word of knowledge, another person gets the word of wisdom to know what to do with it, still another gets a different ability needed in the plan. Isn't that how the Fantastic Four work? Each one of them adds their ability at the right time in order to complete their plan. These abilities are all different ways of listening to God.

"Now you are the body of Christ, and each one of you is a part of it. And in the church God has appointed first of all apostles, second prophets, third teachers, then workers of miracles, also those having gifts of healing, those able to help others, those with gifts of administration, and those speaking in different tongues. Are all apostles? Are all prophets? Are all teachers? Do all work miracles? Do all have gifts of healing? Do all speak in tongues? Do all interpret? But eagerly desire the greater gifts" (1 Corinthians 12:27-30).

Right after Paul challenges us to "eagerly desire the greater gifts" he goes into a section on the importance of love that ends by saying that "these three remain: faith, hope and love."

All these gifts have their place, but most people do not receive every gift. No single gift is more important than any other gift. Nowhere are we told that all Christians have a particular gift. In fact, 1 Corinthians 12 seems to suggest that we all have different gifts, perhaps because we are a team, not a solo operation. You have at least one gift. Are you trying to find it? Have you prayed about it? Have you taken a spiritual gifts survey?

Mr. Fantastic would encourage you to use your gifts "for the common good."

Quest of the Day

1. Read 1 Corinthians 14:1-19.

2. Try the gift of prophesy: simply ask God if there is something He wants you to say to someone, or if

there is an encouragement He wants you to give them. Then share it with them in a note or one-on-one.

3. Ask a couple Christians you know, who are fairly experienced, what spiritual gifts they see in you. Then look for opportunities to use them over the next week.

DAY 31: THE LEAGUE
BY NATHAN MARCHAND

Therefore, since we are surrounded by such a great cloud of
witnesses, let us throw off everything that hinders and the sin
that so easily entangles, and let us run with perseverance the
race marked out for us.
Hebrews 12:1

Strange portals have been opening all over the world,
letting vicious creatures through that are attacking cities.
Superheroes like Batman and the Green Lantern investigate
these happenings, but humanity distrusts these costumed
vigilantes. Indeed, as time goes on, and other crime-fighters
like Superman and Wonder Woman get involved, even the
heroes begin distrusting each other. Some think Batman is
useless because he has no powers. Green Lantern is cocky
and thinks he can handle things on his own. Wonder Woman
doesn't understand how "man's world" operates. The young
Superman has an independent streak in him.

Eventually, they learn these creatures are called
Parademons and are the forerunners of an invasion from the
hellish planet Apokolips and its despotic ruler, Darkseid.
Then, in the face of the alien tyrant's horrific hordes, seven
unlikely allies—Superman, Batman, Wonder Woman, the
Flash, Aqua Man, Green Lantern, and Cyborg—join forces.

With their combined might and powers, they beat back the invaders and seal the portals.

So began DC Comics "New 52" comics in 2011, with the first six issues of *Justice League*, written by Geoff Johns. This comic line rebooted the DC universe with a new continuity. Seminal to this was the origin of the Justice League, the all-star team featuring DC's most powerful and famous heroes. The comic became the New 52's flagship title.

Like the Justice League, Christians are to be united in a common goal. But we so often get fixated on accomplishing our own objectives that we fail to ask fellow believers for help. We even compete with them over ministry opportunities. We forget that we are on the same team, that we have the same goal: to glorify God and share the Gospel of Jesus Christ with the world. Sometimes it takes a huge crisis—a schism in the church, for example—before we realize that we are stronger together than we are apart.

There's a saying that's been floating around that says, "There are no lone wolf Christians." Any believer who thinks he can get by on his own is fooling himself. Just like even the mighty Superman was overwhelmed by the swarms of Parademons, the Devil will pick off any loner Christians. But in the company of fellow believers, there is safety. They can defend each other, pray for each other, and encourage each other, all while striving toward the same destiny.

Besides, it's much more fun to save the world with friends.

Quest of the Day

1. If your church offers Sunday school, pick a class and attend it this Sunday.
2. If your church has small groups, find out what sorts of groups are offered. Attend one that strikes your interest this week.

DAY 32: ARCHENEMY
BY NATHAN MARCHAND

The great dragon was hurled down—that ancient serpent
called the devil, or Satan, who leads the whole world astray.
He was hurled to the earth, and his angels with him.
Revelation 12:9

Batman and the Joker. Superman and Lex Luthor. Iron Man and the Mandarin. The Doctor and the Daleks.

Every hero has a villain in his rogues gallery who is his archenemy. This villain may not be the hero's most powerful enemy, but he serves as the hero's foil, his polar opposite. He is a counterpoint to the hero's beliefs, and vice versa. Their conflicts are more than physical battles: they are wars of ideas.

Batman is stoic and controlled; the Joker is insane and chaotic. Superman is arguably a god who lives to serve mankind; Lex Luthor is a mortal who lives to accomplish his own ends at the expense of others. Iron Man uses science and technology to fight crime; the Mandarin uses magic and superstition to seek world domination. The Doctor believes in the sanctity of all life in the universe; the Daleks believe they are a supreme race and hate all life in the universe.

Whole books could be written that deconstruct these characters' clashing philosophies (I'd probably write a few myself), but that isn't the point. The point is that heroes are brought in sharp relief by their greatest nemeses. What the heroes represent, symbolize, and believe is further accentuated by the villains they fight.

Jesus Christ, despite living a perfect life, had many enemies. It was unavoidable because it is the nature of evil to hate what is good. Jesus clashed with the Pharisees, the Sadducees, and demons. But His greatest nemesis was and is the Devil.

The Devil is known by many names. The Bible calls him Satan, which is derived from the Hebrew word for "adversary." He is also called Lucifer, which was derived from the Latin word for "morning star" (see Isaiah 14:12).

These names give you a hint of his character. If Jesus is pure good, the Devil is pure evil. He was the serpent in the Garden of Eden that led Adam and Eve into sin. He is described as a "red dragon" in Revelation. He made a cosmic bet with God that Job would curse God's name if God stripped Job of his blessings. He is the "father of lies" (John 8:44) and the "accuser of the brethren" (Rev. 12:10).

Revelation says the Devil was an angel who served God until he rebelled against the Almighty. He used his silver tongue to convince one-third of the angelic hosts to side with him. There was a war in Heaven, but the Devil lost and was cast out. Unable to defeat God, he has turned his sights on those made in God's image: mankind.

Yes, not only is he God's enemy, he is *our* enemy. He wants nothing more than to see us destroyed. He and his demons watch us all, learning our every weakness, and then exploiting them. He tempts us to sin and, once we do, he makes us his slaves and puts us in spiritual bondage.

Unfortunately, the Devil isn't a physical being. If he was, we could more easily fight him. The Apostle Paul said, "Our struggle is not against flesh and blood, but against the rulers, against the authorities, against the powers of this dark world and against the spiritual forces of evil in the heavenly realms" (Eph. 6:12). While we may have human enemies, they are but the tools of our true Enemy. We must never lash out at them but use the "spiritual armor" Paul outlines in Ephesians 6:13-18.

In other words, put on your "costume" and get ready for a fight!

Quest of the Day

1. Read Eph. 6:10-18. Pray each piece of the armor of God over yourself.
2. Find a picture of the armor of God (or a knight) online or elsewhere. Post it someplace where you'll see it every day as a reminder to put on your armor. If you're an artist, you could draw it yourself.

DAY 33: BEWARE THE DARK SIDE
BY ERIC ANDERSON

"Why are you still sleeping? Get up and pray so that you will
not fall into temptation."
Luke 22:45

Anakin Skywalker was shocked at what he was hearing. Palpatine knew about his dreams? He knew about the Dark Side of the Force? He even claimed he could help him save Padme. He offered him an opportunity.

"Join me and I will teach you things about the Force the Jedi would never share with you."

He notified Mace Windu about this, who then took three other Jedi with him to interrogate and arrest Palpatine. But the Chancellor could save Padme. Or so he said. So, Anakin left the Jedi temple, went to Palpatine, and joined the Dark Side of the Force, helping Palpatine kill Mace in the process.

Eve faced a similar choice. She was standing near a tree from which she was told not to eat...the one tree in the entire Garden that she should not eat from.

"Why don't you eat from this tree?" the Serpent asked her.

"God told us we would die if we did that."

"No, no. If you eat from this tree, you will be like Him; knowing good from evil."

In other words, God doesn't want you to know something. But I'll share it with you. She took a bite. Adam, her husband and the other half of the first couple, also took a bite. And then life changed for all of humanity.

We all face temptation. It comes from our selfish desires and evolves as we feed them. But temptation doesn't come from God.

"When tempted, no one should say 'God is tempting me.' For God cannot be tempted by evil, nor does he tempt anyone; but each person is tempted when, by his own evil desire, he is dragged away and enticed" (James 1:13, 14).

Satan himself tried to tempt Jesus, who had been fasting for 40 days when the Devil approached Him. He was physically weak. First, Satan tempted Him with the need for strength. Jesus used scripture to block it. Then Satan said, "Jump off this building, God's angels will protect you." Jesus again used Scripture to say, "No." Finally, Satan offered Him the whole world; every kingdom, for the price of worshiping him. Jesus said, "Get away from me!" and again used Scripture to block it.

The enemy tried to tempt Jesus with pride, with challenging God's promises, and with influence in the world. The enemy looks for your biggest weaknesses. And yes, he did even misuse Scripture in his temptation to Jesus. The enemy knows the Bible. Do you?

The best defense against temptation is prayer and scripture. While in the Garden of Gethsemane, Jesus urged the disciples to pray "so that you will not fall to temptation" (Mark 14:38). I have had times when I had to pray to avoid temptation.

The other source is the Bible:

"All Scripture is God-breathed and is useful for teaching, rebuking, correcting and training in righteousness, so that the man of God may be thoroughly equipped for every good work" (2 Timothy 3:16, 17).

About 30 years after Anakin became Darth Vader, he brought his son before Palpatine. The Emperor urged Luke to use his anger about the trap his friends were in to kill Darth Vader and join him.

"Never. I am a Jedi, like my father before me. You have failed, Your Highness."

Jesus went to the cross to defeat sin for you. He died so you could be free from sin and be part of His kingdom. Satan will give you a lot of sin, but he will never die for you. But because of Christ's death, you can resist temptation like Luke did.

Quest of the Day

1. Read Genesis 3 and Matthew 4:1-11.

2. Compare what Adam and Eve experienced after the fall with what Jesus experienced after the Devil left Him. Which is better?

3. Read Hebrews 12:1-6.

DAY 34: THE MOST COMMON TOOL
BY ERIC ANDERSON

...Satan himself masquerades as an angel of light.
2 Corinthians. 11:14

Deception is a common practice among villains. Think about what Sauron did in *Lord of the Rings*. He gave beautiful rings to leaders of men, dwarves, and elves, but then forged another ring to gain control of them. Then he turned the nine kings of men into his lackeys, albeit very powerful lackeys.

Think about Doctor Doom in *Fantastic Four: Rise of the Silver Surfer*. He told the government he wanted to stop the Surfer but, in reality, he was using them to trap the Surfer so that he could use the board and gain its power.

Palpatine in the *Star Wars* prequels had all the Jedi convinced he knew nothing of the Force, when he was in fact the Dark Lord of the Sith.

The Bible warns that the Devil is also a clever deceiver: "But I am afraid that just as Eve was deceived by the serpent's cunning, your minds may somehow be led astray from your sincere and pure devotion to Christ. For if someone comes to you and preaches a Jesus other than the Jesus we preached, or if you receive a different spirit from the one you received, or a different gospel from the one you accepted…" (2 Corinthians 11:3, 4).

Paul goes on to talk about men who are not truly apostles. There were so many attempts at faking apostleship, even with letters, that Paul had to start signing his letters a particular way so that people would know that they were from him.

"For such men are false apostles, deceitful workmen, masquerading as apostles of Christ. And no wonder, for Satan himself masquerades as an angel of light. It is not surprising then, if his servants masquerade as servants of righteousness. Their end will be what their actions deserve" (2 Corinthians 11:13-15).

I heard stories of a man in Mexico who was healing people in the name of "Jesus." After a year or so, all the people would get their ailments back again. The healings didn't last. You see, it wasn't Jesus of Nazareth, the Son of God, whose power he was using. It was a different spiritual master he was serving.

So, what are we to do? How do we know truth from deceit?

"Who is the liar? It is the man who denies that Jesus is the Christ. Such a man is the antichrist—he denies the Father and the Son. No one who denies the Son has the Father; whoever acknowledges the Son has the Father also.

See that what you have heard from the beginning remains in you. If it does, you also will remain in the Son and in the Father" (1 John 2:22-24).

It comes down to two things. First, when listening to a preacher or teacher, discern how they view Jesus. Not just if they think he is "nice" or a "good teacher," but what they really think of Him. Do they trust in Him as their saving Messiah?

Second, internalize the Bible. Here are a few tips about that:

1. **Study scripture.** Memorize it.

2. **Compare Scripture with other Scripture.** Sometimes, in order to understand one part of the Bible, you need to learn from another part of it.

3. **Keep individual verses in context.** Find out what the verses around that verse say and what it all says together.

Deception may be a powerful tool, but having the Holy Spirit is like getting advice from both Yoda, yet far more amazing than the old Jedi Master could ever be!

Quest of the Day

1. Read John 8:31-47.

2. How does Jesus differentiate the liars from the truth-tellers?

DAY 35: GUIDED PRAYER DAY – PRAY FOR NERD/GEEK CULTURE

The nerd/geek culture is largely ignored by the church. Today you will be praying for that subculture, that God will shine His light in it.

1. Pray for the creators of the games, books, comics, movies, and TV shows nerds/geeks love. There are those like Joss Whedon, who are respectful of Christianity. Pray they come to a saving knowledge of Jesus Christ. Just think what God could do with them if they chose to follow Him! Whichever ones are your favorites, pray for them.

2. Pray for the actors involved in movies like the Marvel films and TV shows like *Doctor Who* that they would also come to a saving knowledge of Christ. Pray for the casts of your favorite ones.

3. Pray that those Christians already involved in such productions—like Stephen Lawhead, Alice Cooper, and Jason David Franks, among others—will remain strong in their faith and be shining lights in these industries. They may even face persecution from other Christians, so pray they can withstand the criticism and continue their work.

4. Pray for the film productions of works by Christians, like the *Hobbit* and *Chronicles of Narnia* films, that they will not only be produced but that the Christian themes within them will be preserved.

5. Pray for Christian organizations that reach out to the nerd/geek culture. They've taken on a large task, working in a field that desperately needs workers. These organizations include:

   - Fans For Christ

   - Christian Gamers Guild

   - GameChurch

6. Pray for the conventions in your area, that God will send Christians to be salt and light at them. If you plan to attend one, pray He will use you in that capacity.

7. Pray that, in your interactions with fellow fans, nerds, and geeks, you will conduct yourself as Jesus would. Show those people love. Don't make your faith a secret. Be a visual representation of Christ, in spite of your imperfections.

DAY 36: ONLY YOU CAN TELL YOUR STORY
BY ERIC ANDERSON

"But let the one that boasts boast about this: that they have
the understanding to know me, that I am the Lord, who
exercises kindness, justice and righteousness on Earth, for in
these I delight," declares the Lord Almighty.
Jeremiah 12:24

In the *Doctor Who* episode "Last of the Time Lords,"
the Doctor is being held prisoner by the Master, who has
conquered Earth and is living in an aircraft carrier in the sky.
His body has been aged to show his 900 years of life, so he is
small like an imp and held in a birdcage. Captain Jack
Harkness is also being held prisoner, as is the family of
Martha Jones, the Doctor's companion.

We find Martha Jones coming back to British soil for
the first time in a year. She had been travelling around the
Earth, meeting people. Everyone knows who she is and has
different theories about what she's been doing and what she
will do. Soon after that, the Master captures her, thinking
himself triumphant, as he has destroyed the "weapon" he
thought she was going to use on him.

Then she starts explaining what has really been going
on since she escaped. She has been talking. Not creating a
weapon. Not arming people—well, not with normal weapons,
at least. She has been telling her stories about the Doctor.

About the feats she has seen him accomplish and his impact on her life. Then, at that moment, when all seems lost, all people around the world start thinking and saying his name, "The Doctor." Instantly, everything changes.

We often practice evangelism as one of two extremes. We think of it like a belt. We are so busy telling as many people as possible about Jesus so that we can "gather notches," that we forget the individuals themselves. Or we focus on earning people's respect before telling them and often don't share the Truth with them at all. Sometimes we think "that's the pastor's job, not mine." Quite often we are scared of saying anything. What if we need to be in between?

What if you just took the right moment and told them about your experience with Jesus? Is that hard? You recommend movies, books and games to people, so why not recommend your Savior? What did Jesus tell the man who had been possessed by many demons?

"As Jesus was getting into the boat, the man who had been demon-possessed begged to go with him. Jesus did not let him, but said, 'Go home to your family and tell them how much the Lord has done for you, and how he has had mercy on you.' So the man went away and began to tell in the Decapolis how much Jesus had done for him. And all the people were amazed" (Mark 5:18-20).

Jesus didn't tell him to go bring them all to Him. He didn't tell the man to go and invite them to a weekend-long retreat and convention. He told the man He had healed to go tell his friends and family and share what Jesus had done in his life. Jesus didn't send the man to school or expect him to become a preacher, but just to share his story.

What is your story with Jesus? Have you thought about it?

Quest of the Day

Write your testimony down; just a couple pages. Spend a short time on what you were like before Jesus. Spend a longer time on how you met Him. Then share how your life is different because of Him. Include a couple anecdotes about your significant moments with Him. They could be miracles He did for you (large or small). They might be times when He gave you peace and walked with you through a difficult time.

DAY 37: SHARK REPELLENT BAT-SPRAY
BY NATHAN MARCHAND

…always be prepared to give an answer to everyone who asks
you to give a reason for the hope that you have.
1 Peter 3:15b

Batman has a gadget for everything. No matter how tough a scrape he gets himself into, he has a tool on his utility belt that will save his hide.

Even if he's bitten by a shark. Seriously.

In the opening scene of the 1966 movie *Batman,* starring Adam West as the Caped Crusader and Burt Ward as Robin, the Dynamic Duo fly off in the Batcopter to rescue a commodore who's out to sea in his yacht. Batman climbs down a rope ladder toward the boat. But they quickly learn—as Admiral Akbar says—it's a trap! The yacht disappears and a(n) (obviously rubber) shark bites Batman's leg. Unable to fight the beast off, Batman shouts at Robin to bring him his greatest invention of all time—

Shark Repellent Bat-Spray.

Yes, you read that right.

Robin climbs down the ladder and gives Batman the repellent, with which he sprays the hungry shark. Then it lets go, falls, and—I kid you not—explodes.

Only in the Silver Age of comics could *anyone* get away with such a preposterous and amazing gadget. Because anything with a "Bat-" prefix gets a +10 to its awesomeness.

Now, while we don't have a handy-dandy shark repellent, the Apostle Peter reminds us that we, as Christians, are required to "have an answer...for the hope that you have." People will ask us why we're different from everyone else. Why our morals are better; why we don't succumb to despair as easily; why we're as passionate about our ministries as we are. Some will also question us, perhaps even attack us like a (rubber) shark. In all those instances, we will need to answer their inquiries and/or accusations.

That isn't to say we'll have all the answers. Unlike Batman, we don't have a response for everything. Some questions are just too big and complex to answer. "Why does God allow suffering?" "How can Jesus be fully divine and fully human?" It may seem like a cop-out, but sometimes the only good answer is, "I accept it by faith."

Regardless, don't read your Bible—study it. Ask questions. Seek answers. Read books on apologetics (the discipline of defending the faith). Discuss matters of faith with older, wiser Christians. Garner as much knowledge as you can so you can address these issues when they come up. It will strengthen your own faith and may help persuade others.

Then, just for fun, once you're done making your statement, add, "I'm Batman!"

Quest of the Day

1. Ask your pastor for his recommendations of books to read concerning Christianity. (*Mere Christianity* by C.S. Lewis is a great place to start). There are some recommendations in this book's appendix.
2. Commit to reading at least one of those books, starting this week.

DAY 38: LET THEM LAUGH
BY NATHAN MARCHAND

But do this with gentleness and respect, keeping a clear
conscience, so that those who speak maliciously against your
good behavior in Christ may be ashamed of their slander.
1 Peter 3:16b-17

In *A Christmas Carol* by Charles Dickens, Ebenezer
Scrooge was a man who, as the Muppets sang it, "If they gave
awards for being mean, the winner would be him." He was a
dingy, greedy old man, steeped in bitterness. He wouldn't
even let his clerk, Bob Cratchit, burn some coal in the cold
winter because he didn't want to have to buy more!

Of course, we all know the story of what happened
that fateful Christmas Eve. He was visited by the Spirits of
Christmas Past, Christmas Present, and Christmas Future,
who showed him the error of his ways, and he swore to
reform. No sooner did he awake from his sleep on Christmas
Day than he began his new life. He gave money to charity;
bought a prize turkey for the Cratchits; attended his
longsuffering nephew's dinner; and gave Bob Cratchit a raise.

But such a sudden transformation was unbelievable to
many. As the book closed, Dickens wrote:

*Some people laughed to see the alteration in him, but
he let them laugh, and little heeded them; for he was*

wise enough to know that nothing had ever happened on this globe, for good, at which some people did not have their fill of laughter in the outset; and knowing that such as these would be blind anyway, he thought it quite as well that they would wrinkle their eyes in grins, as have the malady in less attractive forms. His own heart laughed; and that was quite enough for him.

Despite your moral lifestyle, there will be some who will slander you (perhaps it will be *because* of your morality). As I wrote before, it's the nature of evil to hate what is good. But as the Apostle Peter points out, Christians should live in such a way that it shames those slanderers. What good are lies if they don't stick? People will see the slanderers for the villains they are. Perhaps the slanderers will not only be silenced but come to a saving faith themselves once they see the authenticity of your faith.

St. Francis of Assisi said, "Preach the Gospel and, if necessary, use words." Perhaps nowadays he would agree with the saying, "Actions speak louder than words." We must practice what we preach. Then people will see we are genuine, and that will point them to Jesus.

So, always treat everyone—even your naysayers—with the utmost respect. Call them out when you have to, but never stoop to their level. If they don't relent, do what

Scrooge did: "Let them laugh." They're only making fools of themselves.

Quest of the Day

1. Jesus commands His followers to "love [their] enemies." If someone is slandering you because of your faith, repay them by doing something kind for them at least once this week.

2. Pray for the strength to continue doing good, despite the outside pressure.

DAY 39: THE HITCHHIKER'S GUIDE TO WORSHIP
BY ERIC ANDERSON

When they saw him, they worshiped him....
Matthew 28:17

Do you remember your first time watching the original *Star Wars* trilogy straight in one day? Do you recall one or two books that you keep reading again and again because of how good they were? Do you ever go back and relive the glory days of the original Nintendo Entertainment System?

We all have days when we finish a show or game and can't wait to tell people about them. I get like that with a lot of *Doctor Who* episodes. I don't understand how people don't care to watch it!

Shouldn't life with Jesus be like this?

We have this tendency in Christianity to naively, or selfishly, focus on numbers. How big is our church? How many people have we told the Gospel to? We make evangelism a numbers game. How often does that work for us? I have shared my faith many times, but I have yet to lead someone to Jesus. Why?

Earlier this year, I had a new thought from my church. It comes from the Great Commission:

"Then the eleven disciples went to Galilee to the mountain where Jesus had told them to go. When they saw him, they worshiped him; but some doubted. Then Jesus came to them and said, 'All authority in heaven and on earth has been given to me. Therefore go and make disciples of all nations...'" (Matthew 28:16-18).

Did you notice this? First, they obeyed Jesus. They went where He *told* them to go. Not near it. They didn't say, "Well, we like it here in Jerusalem...shouldn't important stuff be in major cities?" They went where they were told. But that isn't the big thing.

Before Jesus gave the Great Commission, they worshiped Him. Could it really be that simple? Could it be that our sharing of Christ should come from our time with Him? To put it another way, do you ever recommend a movie you have never watched? Do you encourage someone to spend $60 on a video game you know nothing about?

Think about the moment in the movie *Hitchhikers Guide to the Galaxy* when Trillian is showing Arthur around the ship. She tells him about the galley first. She shows him the laser knife that toasts bread, and the machine that creates whatever food you are craving. She cannot stop talking about this adventure in space. Why? Because she has been there! She has travelled around in the Heart of Gold, and seen a portion of what was out there. Her world had been opened up, and she had to tell someone about it.

I'm sure you recommend books, TV shows, games, and other things to friends. Great. Now, the next time you have an amazing experience with Jesus, tell someone about it! Sharing Jesus with people who don't know Him shouldn't come like a telemarketer trying to make a quota. Nobody likes telemarketers. We turn down telemarketers simply because they are telemarketers (and because they're normally annoying). But you listen to your friends. When one of your friends finds a great product, and is excited about it, you ask them about it and you try it yourself.

As you worship Christ and spend time with Him, He'll reveal new ideas, new adventures, and new directions to you. This will lead to people seeing Him in you and then opportunities for you to share. Don't be a telemarketer. Be a friend on an amazing journey. Then, you can invite your friends to join the journey. Ultimately, Arthur and Trillian went back on the journey in space. They didn't spend so much time telling people about it that they missed it. They could have done that. They could have stayed on Earth and tried to tell everyone about traveling through space, but that would have taken them away from the journey. Enjoy the journey with Jesus, and that will lead to opportunities to share Him.

Don't be a salesman of a journey. Be an explorer inviting people into the journey.

Quest of the Day

1. Spend a few extra moments alone with God today, praying and reading your Bible. Give Him some time to speak to you.

2. Ask Jesus if there is a particular friend He wants you to tell about your journey with Him. Then, find a time over coffee or a meal to share what He is doing for you in your life right now. Don't push it. Just let it come naturally.

DAY 40: GUIDED PRAYER DAY - PRAYER FOR MISSIONS

1. Pray for the missionaries your church supports. If you have any newsletters or prayer alerts from them, use those to know what to pray. If not, check with your church and see if they know of any current prayer requests.

2. Pray for Christian organizations that express mercy and fight injustice. Here are a few:

    - International Justice Mission (fighting human trafficking)

    - Mercy Ships (hospital ships that go to places with few doctors)

    - Living Water International (building wells for villages with no safe water)

    - World Hope International (skills classes, counseling, etc.)

    - Compassion International (caring for kids in poverty)

3. Pray for the 10/40 window. This section of the world—10 degrees north to 40 degrees north—from Africa through Asia has the largest number of people groups who do not have a representation of Christ (i.e. churches and accessible Bibles in their own

language) and the smallest percentage of missionaries. Pray for:

- "Workers for the Harvest" (people to go share Christ)
- Accessibility to the Word of God in their own languages
- Strength and protection for Christians in areas of hostility
- Opportunities to share Christ
- Christian radio broadcasts to be effective
- Dreams/visions/miracles to lead people to Christ

4. Pray that both terrorists and those who persecute Christians would have "Saul to Paul" experiences, and come to Christ. What if the leaders of organizations like Al-Qaida came to Christ and changed their ways? Ask God to reveal Himself to them and for them to become followers of Christ.

5. Pray for the researchers in Antarctica. Pray that Christ would reveal Himself to them and that they would have safety in dangerous conditions.

6. Choose a particular non-denominational missions organization to pray for. Here are a few organizations

you may want to keep in prayer. You might find prayer requests on their websites:

- Youth with A Mission (20,000 fulltime staff, discipleship schools in at least 1,000 locations worldwide). (www.ywam.org)
- Project Partner with Christ (www.projectpartner.org). Serving the needs of China.
- Africa Inland Mission (AIM)
- Wycliffe International (translating the Bible into local languages) (www.wycliffe.org)
- Send International (www.send.org)

7. Pray for Voice of the Martyrs as they seek to cooperate with believers in areas of high instances of persecution. Pray that these believers would have wisdom, strength, and courage.

8. Pray for Jerusalem, that many there would come to Christ. This can be a volatile city (but one well worth visiting!). "Pray for the peace of Jerusalem: 'May those who love you be secure. May there be peace within your walls and security within your citadels" (Psalm 122:6).

DAY 41: JESUS AND MYSTERY, INC.
BY ERIC ANDERSON

I am sending you out like sheep among wolves. Therefore be
as shrewd as snakes and as innocent as doves.
Matthew 10:16

In our last two days together, we are looking at a couple of verses from Matthew 10. This chapter shows training that Jesus did with His disciples before sending them out in twos to take His message everywhere they went. There is a lot in this chapter, so we are going to focus on two passages. Today, we will talk about verse 16:

"I am sending you out like sheep among wolves. Therefore be as shrewd as snakes and as innocent as doves."

Now wait a minute. Sheep are meat; for wolves, anyway. And sheep aren't particularly amazing fighters, are they? Do the sheep in Settlers of Catan ever fight off the robber? They aren't particularly smart or capable, either. If they fall over, they need help being righted, or else they die. They are dependent animals. So why would Christ tell us to be like them?

Because they are trusting animals. They always follow to the call of their shepherd. Jesus wants us to come when He calls.

Now, what does it mean to be "shrewd and innocent"? The word "shrewd" in the original Greek is *phronomoi.* It is normally translated as "wisdom," and comes up in seven other passages in the New Testament. The base word refers to a "personal perspective regulating outward behavior." It sometimes is translated as "prudent" or "sensible." This emphasizes a wisdom focused on caution rather than on skill or intelligence. The word for "innocent" is *akeraioi.* This particular word comes up only a couple other times in the New Testament. It refers to being unmixed, pure. It means you don't have any evil within you.

This reminds me of Scooby-Doo and the gang from Mystery Incorporated. A bunch of meddling kids stopping scammers in elaborate costumes. Who doesn't love this show? You have Freddy, the leader of the group who loves adventure. Then Velma the geek. She is always investigating, researching, and figuring out the details. Daphne is always getting into trouble, but keeps the group grounded. We like knowing that a member of the group is "normal." Then you have Shaggy, the "scaredy-cat" who never stops eating. Finally, there's the joy of the team, Scooby-Doo, the dog who sorta talks and makes wild sandwiches and will do anything for his Scooby snacks.

Despite how quickly Freddy and Velma want to investigate, you always had the caution of Shaggy and Scooby. The gang would never back down from a mystery, but they wouldn't let the world stop them, either. There was no buying them out with treasure (ok, so maybe Scooby and Shaggy would consider being paid off in food). They approached everything as peaceably as possible, so they never used weapons (although Velma loved to set traps).

Paul put this another way in Romans 16:19-20:

"Everyone has heard about your obedience, so I am full of joy over you; but I want you to be wise about what is good, and innocent about what is evil. The God of peace will soon crush Satan under your feet."

Does that describe Mystery, Inc? They take risks to help people they don't even know. They don't try to harm the people they catch doing this. Well, not by cartoon physics, at least. The "meddling kids" didn't always look before they leapt, but we should allow the Holy Spirit to guide us and to be that personal perspective that regulates outward behavior.

Let's be the "pesky kids" filled with the One Who binds the enemy!

Quest of the Day

1. What is a behavior in your life right now that needs to be regulated from a biblical viewpoint?
2. Read Matthew 10.
3. How does verse 16 fit into the message as a whole?
4. Journal about all of these.

DAY 42: I DARE YOU TO DO BETTER
BY NATHAN MARCHAND

Whoever finds his life will lose it, and whoever loses his life
for my sake will find it.
Matthew 10:39

"You like being the only genius-level repeat offender
in the Midwest?" asked Capt. Pike.

"Maybe I love it," replied James T. Kirk, still bloodied
from the bar room brawl Pike rescued him from.

"So your dad dies, and you can settle for something
less than an ordinary life. But you feel like you were meant
for something better. Something special. Enlist in Starfleet."

Kirk laughed at him. Pike told Kirk he could become
an officer in four years and have his own ship in eight, but he
wouldn't listen, so Pike stood to leave. "Your father was
captain of a starship for twelve minutes. I dare you to do
better." He walked out, telling him the shuttle with new
recruits left in the morning.

Kirk then rode a motorcycle out to where a starship
was being constructed. He saw what he could have. A
destiny, a purpose. So, he went to the shuttle yard, walked up
to Pike and said, "Four years? I'll do it in three!"

These scenes from the 2009 *Star Trek* film show a
young Kirk with much potential, but no direction. He was

apathetic, willing to settle for an aimless life of carousing and troublemaking. Until Capt. Pike reminded him he could do better. He goes on to save Earth from a dastardly Romulan by the end of the film.

In Matthew 10, Jesus sent His 12 disciples out to minister to nearby villages. He gave them many instructions. They would do great works, but they would also face opposition and persecution. However, He promised they would be empowered by their faith for the tasks at hand. It culminated with Jesus saying, "Whoever finds his life will lose it, and whoever loses his life for my sake will find it." It's the most frequent saying of Jesus recorded in the Gospels.

Jesus isn't just talking about dying for the sake of the Gospel. I think it's also about finding your purpose. Our lives belong to God. Before we fully dedicated ourselves, our lives were like Kirk's: menial. But once we chose to follow Christ, He not only gave us salvation, He gave us a purpose: to use our talents and gifts to serve and glorify Him. Once Kirk decided to join Starfleet, he had purpose in life, a mission. Read the Great Commission in Matthew 28:16-20. That's our mission.

We are more than sinners saved by grace. We are saints with a mission. We are officers in the Lord's army.

The last 42 days you've been reading this devotional have been part of God's preparation and training to use you for His good purposes. It's one reason why Eric and I wrote this book.

Now, go fight the good fight (1 Timothy 6:12)!

<u>Quest of the Day</u>

1. Read Matthew 28:16-20 and Acts 1:1-11.

2. Pray for God to reveal to you a specific cause He wants you involved in (pro-life movement, helping the homeless, etc.) It should be something you are passionate about. Find ways to get involved with it. If you already are, do it wholeheartedly!

Anderson and Marchand

APPENDIX: RECOMMENDED RESOURCES

Fruit of the Spirit: 48 Bible Studies for Individuals or Groups
(Published by Zondervan, authored by Phyllis J. Le Peau, Jack
Kuhatschek, Jacalyn Eyre, Stephen Eyre, Peter Scazzero)
Zondervan Bible Dictionary/Zondervan Bible Encyclopedia
The Books of the Bible Series (Published by Biblica)
> The Bible without chapter/verse numbers
Daring Greatly by Brene Brown
> Exploring the need for vulnerability in leadership.
Orthodoxy by G.K. Chesteron
Epic by John Eldredge
> Grand story of God's involvement in our world.
Waking the Dead by John Eldredge
> The glory of a heart fully alive
Beautiful Outlaw by John Eldredge
> Experiencing the playful, disruptive, and extravagant
> personality of Jesus
Celebration of Discipline: The Path to Spiritual Growth by Richard J.
> Foster
Mere Christianity by C.S. Lewis
The Weight of Glory by C.S. Lewis
The Screwtape Letters by C.S. Lewis
Reaching Out by Henri Nouwen
> 3 Movements in the Spiritual Life
Christianity Today
Relevant Magazine
www.biblegateway.com

Anderson and Marchand

ACKNOWLEDGEMENTS

There are many people who contribute to a book's creation beyond the author(s). Even a small self-published devotional like this wouldn't be possible without help from others.

First, a huge thanks to the creators, actors, and producers who worked on all the amazing material we drew from for our analogies. Maybe you didn't intend for your stories to hold such meaning, but we believe that Truth (with a capital T) can be found anywhere. You are what make nerdy/geeky fandoms possible. Thank you again!

A special thanks to the members of Fans For Christ (FFC), especially those in the Facebook group. When we asked for ideas for analogies, you were quick and creative in your responses. We wish we could remember all of your specific names so we could list them here. You may not remember making contributions, but your influence is scattered throughout this book.

A special thanks to Nick Hayden (www.WorksofNick.com) and Kim Huther for editing this book. We can't thank you enough!

Anderson and Marchand

ABOUT THE AUTHORS

Eric "Mister" Anderson is a substitute teacher by day and the founder of Nerd Chapel by night. He attended Taylor University Fort Wayne (where he met Nathan) and earned a B.A. in Biblical Studies and Christian Education. He lives in Fruitport, Michigan. His first ministry was a Christian club at his middle school. He graduated from Youth with a Mission Discipleship Training School and has been on many missions trips. His other ministries include leading Bible studies and handling church tech (sound/lighting for services). You can find more of his insights on nerd-dom and faith at www.nerdchapel.blogspot.com or at www.facebook.nerdchapel.com. You can also find him on YouTube by searching "Nerd Chapel." *42* is his first published work.

"Super" Nathan Marchand is from northeastern Indiana. Homeschooled from an early age, he discovered his talent for writing in sixth grade English. He has loved speculative fiction since his dad introduced him to the original *Star Trek* at age three. He attended Taylor University Fort Wayne, earning a B.A. in professional writing. He's worked as a reporter in a small town, a feature writer for www.Examiner.com, and as a freelance writer, among other things. His first novel, *Pandora's Box*, was published in 2010 by Absolute XPress. He's also the co-creator of the ongoing fantasy serial, *Children of the Wells* (www.ChildrenoftheWells.com), and the host of his own YouTube show, "But I Digress…." When not writing, he enjoys other creative endeavors like photography, acting, ballroom dancing, and occasionally saving the world. His website is www.NathanJSMarchand.com.

Made in the USA
Middletown, DE
15 July 2015